Ron Ritco

Kill Me If You Can

Ron Ritco

Suite 300 - 990 Fort St
Victoria, BC, V8V 3K2
Canada

www.friesenpress.com

First Edition — 2017

Kelsey Ritco-Day
Translator

Mike Klemak
Editor

Sandy Cochlan
Artist

ISBN
978-1-5255-1052-6 (Hardcover)
978-1-5255-1053-3 (Paperback)
978-1-5255-1054-0 (eBook)

1. *BIOGRAPHY & AUTOBIOGRAPHY, PERSONAL MEMOIRS*

Distributed to the trade by The Ingram Book Company

TABLE OF CONTENTS

Kill Me If You Can

INTRODUCTION

THIS IS MY JOURNEY

This is my story, my journey. It begins early on in my life and describes a number of experiences that I have had. Unbelievable and unexplainable as some may be, they are the truth. I ask you to be open-minded. There are many experiences I have had that you may scoff at, but I ask you to think about magical thinking, fantasy, metaphysics, and quantum physics. There is much in this world that most of us don't fully understand. I come from and have a wonderful family; we have lived a lot of life, have seen many things, done a lot, travelled some, and learned.

It is not for any of us to question the life experiences of another. My father-in-law believed in many things and many worlds. He had an open mind, an open heart, and a very curious and discerning spirit. He fought in the second world war; he saw death and he appreciated that there are many things that can be seen, felt, and experienced. Those he did not question; he raised his children to be like-minded, and they have raised their children to be open minded about all experience! I was given the opportunity to have his daughter as my wife for thirty-seven years.

I will miss her always.

I am grateful that we all remain a close family and I appreciate those who understand and support me in my endeavors as I go through life. I know they appreciate my open heart, my compassion, and my love for other human beings.

As you read through these pages, imagine walking with me through my life: put yourself in my shoes, in my mind, in my dreams, and in my visions. It is a journey, a trip, and I am still here to talk to anyone about my life and experiences. I believe I have much to offer, if only to be a smiling face, a hug, a friend, a confidante.

Please drink in the idea of life with the many twists and turns: moments of complete awareness, life without barriers, the idea of more than a two or three dimensional world, with its judgments and biases. Expand your thinking to a place where you can see, feel, dream and visualize the unknown, the unexplainable, the bizarre, and the otherworldly. If you can, you may just find the freedom to LIVE!

I want to say thank you for those people who have contributed to this work, to their time and effort, their talent and artistic ability. Thank you for believing in me, for it is I who also believe and support you!

Our old world is changing, there are many who are caught up in the material and the new technologies that exist today. As I watch and observe, I have a deep sadness that comes over me at times for the loss of connection between people, the loss of connection to the spiritual, and the loss of connection to the potential of all human beings who exist today. I thank God that I was born and lived during a time when we were encouraged to use our imagination, to believe in other ideas, and not succumb to religious dogma and restriction. We were encouraged to connect to nature, we were encouraged to be independent, strong, responsible, and to know ourselves at the deepest possible level. I know that it takes time, maturity, and life experience and, as this book clearly shows, there were a lot of knocks and bumps along the way, but here I am, now a senior who appreciates and loves every moment of every day. Even though I carry sadness and loss with me, I know it is my life's purpose to continue to the next chapter... whatever form that takes.

CHAPTER ONE

DISCOVERING THE WORLD

Since I was a young boy I have experienced many unexplained phenomenon. The following pages contain a description of my journey, my life, and my many experiences. They are unexplainable, unbelievable, and otherworldly, but they are mine.

Every word you will read is the truth of my life!

I also want to remind everyone I was raised on a farm in Grand Forks, British Columbia, Canada. We were kids who learned early on in life that, in order to survive, everyone had to work hard and pitch in. To put food on the table, everyone had to contribute and be responsible, It was not an easy life, but one that I appreciate because it made me the man I am today.

And so we begin!

One of the earliest memories I have is when I was four or five years old. It was a hot summer day and I lived on our farm in Grand Forks. The small house was cozy with my mom, my dad George, my older brother George Jr., and my older sister Robin all living there.

It was a beautiful day, one where the sun was shining and if there was a cloud in the sky, we couldn't see it. Being rambunctious farm kids, opportunities to be outside on a warm day were looked forward to with enthusiasm. We decided to venture to the hay shed to climb on the poles that spanned from one side of the barn to the other. We were all jumping and playing and leaping down into the loose hay pile, laughing and having fun.

At some point, I fell backwards onto the hay pile. As the warm, musty hay cushioned my fall, I laughed with the abandon that only children know. I was about to get up again when I noticed that, between my left hand and my chest, there was a three-prong hay fork that was facing upwards. I pulled it out of the hay and said to Robin, "I'm going to move the fork."

I put the fork by the edge of the hay pile and pushed its tines down into the hay. Even at that young age I realized if I would have fallen four inches to my left, the fork would have gone through mine or my siblings' chest. We could easily have been killed. At that age, it's rare to have the presence of self to think outside of the moment, but it stuck in my mind that *this* was something to remember.

I didn't think of that potentially fatal fork until the next bizarre incident that happened in my youth. It was 1956, my dad was plowing the field east of the old farmhouse. He was going back and forth in the field, about a hundred feet from the CPR Railroad.

My brother George Jr. and I were running along the ditch to the left of the plow, trailing our dad by a couple hundred feet. He'd always made sure to drive that lesson home. *The plow isn't something to play around.* Out from the unplowed side of the furrow came some type of earthworm or snake. To this day I'm still not sure what exactly it was.

This unidentifiable invertebrate was about sixteen inches long and two inches thick. It was white and black in two alternating stripes: a couple inches of black, a couple inches of white, then black for the remainder of its body. It was in front of us in the furrow and it was moving amazingly fast along the ground. It traveled about thirty feet in the furrow, then submerged into the soft plowed dirt, disappearing completely. George Jr. and I dug for it with the reckless abandon that only the truly inquisitive can espouse, but there was no trace of it.

I have never seen anything like it since. Searching in books and biology texts has never revealed anything similar. Often I've thought to myself, *it must be some undiscovered type of worm or snake and there must be more than one... how many actually live in that field?* Everytime I plowed the fields of that farm I looked for another, but I never came across one again. Again, something told me to record the moment and never forget it.

At nine years old, my brothers, Ken and Dale became the newest members of our family. My Dad had shown me how to drive the '48 Ford 8N Tractor. My chores consisted of me cutting hay with the ancient mower and raking it all up with the old horse rake. Our farm of thirty-eight acres had eighteen acres of Ponderosa Pine trees on the west side.

One day, I was driving through the pine trees in fourth gear and going about fifteen miles per hour. It was fun to see how fast I could go between the trees. I made a sharp turn to my left and the tractor went up on two wheels. I slid off the seat and was hanging on to the steering wheel for dear life. My feet were being caught by the back tractor wheel. I knew if I let go of the steering wheel the tractor tire would run over me. Somehow with my other hand I pulled the steering wheel to the right. The tractor fell back onto all four wheels and I managed to pull myself back onto the seat and push the throttle down. The tractor slowed and finally came to a stop. My feet and ankles were beat all to hell, but by some miracle, nothing was broken.

I did not tell my Mom and Dad what I did, as I knew I would get the strap, either from my Dad's belt, or my Mom's ironing cord (which, used just for that purpose, hurt more than the belt). Once again, I felt I had experienced something extraordinary and escaped death.

It was becoming clear that, even before the age of ten, I had played *Nicky Nine Doors* on death's house without being caught, and was witnessing some things that I am sure few people get to see in their entire lives...or choose not to talk about it when they do.

At ten years old, I used to love to run across our field. Whether it was through the tall grass, in amongst the trees, or out in the open, I would run. There was an old, rotten water flume with the boards practically falling apart. One day, I jumped over the flume and I landed on a 3-4-inch rusty nail; it went completely through my foot. My Dad heard my screams as I pulled the board from my foot, affixed by the nail. Dad arrived just as I removed the spike and carried me over to the house. I wasn't bleeding too bad, so Mom poured iodine on it, which seemed like the cure for everything in those days. It burned like hell, but after about a week or so, I was mobile again, running through the field. I decided to stay away from the flumes after that, fearing the inevitability of another iodine treatment.

The electronic age began in 1958 and Dad bought a black and white t.v. We were so excited. *Yes, a television!* We also had a telephone which was on a party line with ten neighbors. When the line was clear we could use the phone. Sometimes the neighbors would listen in, but at least we had one. Our farm was one of the earlier places to have electricity and that was a luxury.

That summer, George and I found a hornet's nest in the ground. We got a can of spray paint and would spray the bees as they came out of the hole. This worked well for a few seconds until the spray stopped. The insects poured out of the hole and George and I fled at a dead run, trying to outrun the hornets. They stung the heck out of my face and the rest of my body. We decided it wasn't as much fun as we thought it would be.

Mom and Dad left town on a trip and George, being the leader, decided we should build a raft. It was ten feet long and six feet wide. George rigged a pole and extended it out the front. When it got dark, George lit a lamp and hung it on the pole. We got on and pushed it out. It was not long before we hit the first set of rapids. We laughed and hung on as the raft accelerated. Down the river in the dark, we went about a mile and a half. We were flying down the river when we got to a sharp bend. We hit the bank and got off as the raft floated away, the lamp still hanging on the pole. We laughed and walked home a mile and a half.

George told his friend that we had a club. The neighbor kids who were ten to twelve years old wanted to join. George told them they had to pass the initiation test to become a member. The kids asked George if they could take the test. George agreed and got our dad's hand saw and we headed out to our forest on the west end of the farm. George told his friend Mickey, "all you have to do is climb this twenty foot tree and hang on. I will cut it down, but you cannot cry. Then you can be in the club."

Robin and I were watching as George cut the tree down. The tree tipped over with Mickey hanging on for his dear life and slammed into the ground. Mickey clawed his way out of the treetop, crying his eyes out. George walked up to him and said, "Mickey, you cried, so you're not in the club. You will have to try again another day." This was one of the most hilarious things that summer as kid after kid tried to pass the test. By the end of the summer, no one had passed his test. George told them that he, Robin, and I had easily passed the test, but we never attempted it.

Next we decided to find a steep hill and take the old baby buggy to go for a ride. I remember climbing in and George sending me off down the hill by the house with George and Robin laughing. The hill was rough and the buggy would never turn when it was supposed to and I would go flying. There was always a new adventure and summer was the most fun. Jumping off the train bridge into the river and swimming and tubing, picking huckleberries, fishing, hot dog roasts, and fresh corn on the cob with homemade butter as well as homemade ice cream. It was a great time to be one of the seven children in my family.

At fourteen, I decided to quit school. I had been raised to work hard, earn a good living, and be responsible for the needs of the family. Going to school was just getting in the way and didn't seem that important at the time. I went to work for the local farmers. My job was pushing a hoe and changing sprinklers. After my work day, I would come home to help with farm duties. Just because you had a job did not mean chores at home didn't need to be done! I took it all in stride: it was the way of life.

During the winter of my fifteenth year, my two friends and I were walking up a steep hill to my place. Despite the snow, cars frequented the road, so we'd walk single file and the right hand side next to a three-foot high snowbank. This one car came flying up the hill; the headlights suddenly illuminating us from behind, so we stepped as far over as we could. I was in the back of our group, concentrating on putting one foot in front of the other. With no warning, the car hit me! I flew up the bank about twenty feet and I remember specifically landing on the wallet in my back pocket. The car never slowed, but continued up the hill oblivious of what had occurred.

It took a few minutes for me to catch my breath and hobble down the road. We were all cursing the car and driver since it hadn't stopped or returned to see if I was okay. I was in a lot of pain, but eventually made it home. The pain was so intense that the next day I looked to see if I was black and blue, but I was the colour I'd always been. After that night, whenever a car came behind me, I would turn and look at it, mentally daring the driver to hit me. I would prepare myself to jump up on the bank if my dare was accepted. No driver seemed up to the task of repeating what had happened that winter. I knew I was lucky and that I easily could have been killed. I also knew that these types of occurrences appeared to be a common theme in my young life.

Years later, I was at home unhooking a three-point plow one night after work. I was between the plow and the tractor, which was still running, As I started unhooking it, the power shaft grabbed my T-shirt and started pulling me towards it. I grabbed the fender of the tractor and held on as my shirt was being ripped off my back. In the midst of that struggle between the plow and myself, I wondered if I was going to get out of this. Luckily, the shirt was pulled in tatters from my back, but I knew that if the shirt hadn't torn, I would have been pulled in and killed.

Now, I don't consider myself different or strange compared to most people, but as far back as I can remember, whenever I would go to sleep, moments would pass before I would open my eyes and find myself looking down at my body. I didn't know why this would happen or what was going on. Sometimes I would see myself and my friends, hanging out somewhere talking about cars or music. The weekend would come, I would meet my friends downtown, the conversation would start, and I immediately recognized that everything was being repeated from my dream earlier in the week. I would often wonder and ask myself, *is this something that happens to everybody or just me?* Of course, something inside me would say, *don't bring it up or talk about it to parents or friends, as I might not like what they have to say.* Something inside me insisted that most people either don't experience the same thing or are simply not aware of it. So I began to feel like I was different from everyone else, which for a young person is not necessarily a good thing. Fearing what people would think, I kept these dreams to myself, and continued to have the premonitions, predictions, and out-of-body experiences that I knew were unique to me.

CHAPTER TWO

TEENAGERS

In 1964, George worked for some farmers and also as a cook and waiter. Somehow he saved enough money to buy a fridge. This was something new to us. A place where you could put anything in it and it would keep everything cool. At the time, a fridge was a luxury and it was expensive. George eventually headed for Vancouver to work. He became an orderly, then a registered nurse, and then got his bachelor degree in nursing.

In 1966 it was pretty common for most people to drink and drive. If you were pulled over, as long as you could walk the white line, you weren't charged, but the RCMP would take your liquor, and that was the biggest loss.

My friend Bernie Cole and I were on a road trip, out having fun across the line, in Curlew, Washington, exactly ten miles from the border. Acting as most sixteen year-olds did in that day, we had been drinking for hours, and were both so loaded we needed to hang onto each other to make it to our car. Despite our lack of sobriety, we were determined to get back across the border into Canada.

"We'll never make the border," I slurred into Bernie's ear. We had ten miles to go before it closed.

"You just tell me what the signs say." Bernie's plan was, because he couldn't clearly see the road signs, I would read them off and he would be able to speed as fast he could to take the corners. He figured that the faster he could go around the corners, the faster we would get to the border on time.

The first sign read 25 mph and we skinned the tires coming around it and almost piled up. The next sign was 45 mph, which converted in Bernie's mind to 70 or faster. We kept going, somehow making it around the corners.

Bernie was now averaging over 60 mph when I said, "twenty five." He was going along and figured we were doing great up until then, accelerating as we went, but wasn't expecting the sudden sharp curve.

The next thing we knew, we hit a rock wall on the wrong side of the road on an angle. It chewed up the left side of the car, the windshield blew out, we spun around three or four times, then went shooting over the bank towards the river. Bernie hit the brakes, put the car in low gear, and we flew back onto the road, landing crossways.

What the hell are we going to do now, I thought. The front fender was bent around the front wheel, so that became our first course of action. We took the jack and pried the fender away so Bernie could steer the car.

With a car that could now turn, we started the ignition and got back in the right lane. With me continuing to call out road signs, we made it to the border just in time. The Customs Officer looked at the front bumper and the driver's side panelling and said, "what the hell happened to your car?"

Bernie was pretty quick on his feet, especially while drunk. He looked at him and said, "it's looked like this for weeks." Even though we didn't think the Customs Officer believed us for one moment, he let us cross the border.

We figured we were home free, back in Canada and on the road to Grand Forks. No sooner had we arrived back in town when the Mounties pulled us over and took Bernie's keys away. We took that as a win. We were back in Canada in one piece and hadn't been arrested. Bernie and I walked a little way down the road until the Mounties were gone, and Bernie turned to me with a twinkle in his eye.

"Might as well go back," he laughed and said, "I have another set of keys."

As the saying goes, *you just can't keep a good man down*. So, we returned and got into the vehicle. The car was more or less totaled, but we had hit a rock wall at 70 mph and lived to talk about it. If I was a cat, I'd have lost count with how many lives I had used up already.

CHAPTER THREE

THE HALO OVER THE GRAVE

The following year found little change in the wisdom of teenagers. It was typical for Friday nights to be hanging out with my friend Arnie. We went out that night, found a bootlegger, and bought some beer. The next step was finding somewhere to hang out and drink without being caught. We drove into the cemetery where the local cops rarely patrolled, minimizing the chance of anyone taking our beer, which was the most important factor to consider.

We drove to the cemetery and pulled onto the access road. Like any cemetery at night, it was dark and foreboding, the headstones sticking up all around us. Like most kids, this made the whole experience more exciting, more of an adventure. We weren't saying much to each other as we explored the foreboding grounds. Arnie and I opened our first can and I busied myself looking out the window at different gravesites. A certain slab of stone caught my eye approximately eight to ten feet away from the front fender of Arnie's truck.

There was this beautiful, glowing light emanating from the grave, a halo that was one inch thick and a foot above the grave. It was glowing an orange-tinged light, shining twelve inches wide. I was fascinated by this beautiful phenomenon, but since Arnie hadn't spoken up, I kept quiet.

Out of the blue, Arnie turns and says, "Ron, do you see anything over there?"

"Why, what do you see?" I asked to make sure he was referencing the same thing. I didn't want to admit that I was seeing an ethereal halo and have Arnie think I was crazy if he was looking at something else entirely.

Arnie pointed out the windshield, "There's a halo over that grave!"

"I see it too!" I admitted.

Both of us decided together, that this is too much to comprehend for either of us. We weren't sure what it was, and didn't want to stick around to find out more. Arnie quickly turned the key, hoping against hope that the 1952 Ford wouldn't decide to be difficult and leave us stranded. Our prayers were answered, as the truck started on the first try and Arnie backed us out of the cemetery. By the time I remembered that we'd opened our beer, it was warm and still clutched in my hand.

That same year, my friend Joe asked me where I got my money from, so I told him I was working changing sprinklers and hoeing for the farmers. I also cut, raked, and baled hay and raised a few hogs. "Hogs?" Joe asked.

"Yes," I said. "I sell them and make eighty bucks." Joe asked where I get the hogs from. I told him that I bought them from a hog farmer for fifteen dollars each. Joe asked me if I'd ever gone out and coon-hunted them (which meant stealing). "No," I replied, "but an old timer told me how they stole weaner pigs. First you need a two man team." At this point, I knew Joe would go along with the idea. We found a barn with piglets and their mother gently sleeping with a heat lamp on them.

"What now?" Joe asked.

"You crawl over the low wall and just walk slowly in front of the sow."

"Why don't you go in?" Joe demanded. I told him that when the piglets walked by, I would put one in each sack. Joe jumped in. The mother woke up and started to chase Joe. She had her mouth wide open and was chasing Joe at a dead run. Around and around they went as I rooted Joe on. I reached in and grabbed a weaner pig, put it in the sack, and tied it. That sow was really pissed off, and I could see Joe slowing down. I yelled for Joe to run. I saw a chance and grabbed another pig. I put it in the sack and tied it.

I looked back and saw that Joe was still ahead of the sow. Joe screamed, "I can't get a hold of her!" So I grabbed another pig and just held it, giving Joe a chance to bail over the wall. I grabbed the pig and Joe vaulted right over the wall. He landed on the floor and I let go of the piglet. The mother sow placed her front feet on the wall and she was reaching out trying to bite our heads off. We grabbed the weaner pigs, put them over our shoulders and walked away.

Joe turned to me, "I'm never going to do that again."

"Joe," I said, "I didn't realize you could run so fast. You could be an Olympic runner." His face turned the colour of the pigs.

CHAPTER FOUR

THOSE FEELINGS INSIDE

I've previously mentioned about the experiences I have with my dreams, where I have a dream about my friends, what we are doing and saying to each other, and when we get together the next day or later that week, it's at the exact location, with the same people, and the same conversations take place.

Well, during my life, whenever the telephone would ring at home, I would have this feeling about who it was and what they were calling about. It was disconcerting at times, because the news wasn't always good.

One night, Dad, Mom, and I were at home on the farm when the telephone started ringing, I knew right away it was my Uncle Pete. I also knew he was going to tell my Dad that my Grandpa had passed away. I kept quiet, but when my Dad got off the phone he told my Mom and I that his Dad had passed away. A cold sweat dripped down my back, but I didn't tell my parents about my premonition.

My dreams have always been in vivid color, are very realistic, but I never fully understood what they meant. When I was younger, I didn't know about premonitions or predictions. I had never heard of Edgar Cayce in those days. I remember times in my dream state looking for a calendar, something to tell me when this was actually going to happen. I never found one. I only saw parts of the situation and knew on a deep level that I was witnessing things I had no control over!

Throughout my life there have been many occasions where I either see or know who is on the phone, who is coming over, what is about to happen or be said. I was never sure if everyone did that, or if it was just me. I assumed that they must, but no one was willing to talk about it openly, so instinctively I didn't either. I didn't always like being this way, because everything I saw and experienced wasn't necessarily pleasant or good news and, more often than not, it was bad. Often I've considered it a burden and a curse rather than a gift.

Who wants to be the bearer of bad news?

CHAPTER FIVE

DEATH AT THE RIVER

In January, 1966, my brother Ken, myself, Clim Anthony, Jerry Anthony, Larry Makoff, and Alex Waykin were hanging out driving around town in Ken's 1956 Ford. Around 7:00 pm Ken drove into our yard at home to let me out of the car; I had to work the next morning driving skidder for Zibbin

Contracting (my job was to skid logs into the landing then other guys would cut the trees into lengths and haul them to the sawmill). I was getting out of the car when Larry shouts, "Ron, you have to come with us."

I said, "I'm home, and I have to work tomorrow. I'm not going!"

Larry levelled a look at me, "you *have* to come with us." He was almost begging me to come. Finally, I relented and got back into the car, figuring another hour or so would still leave me enough time to get home and get to bed.

We left our place, heading toward Alex's place, since he also wanted to get dropped off. Larry turned to Alex, "you have to come too." Alex saw the same thing I had glimpsed in Larry's eyes and agreed to come. We turned left at Plant's Corner and started down the old, narrow road to go to Gilpin, where Larry lived.

We came down the hill, the road frozen with six inch ruts. Ken was keeping it in low gear, navigating the icy decline. Just as we came around the bend of the river, the car jumped out of the ruts, even though Ken hadn't intended it. The car started heading over the bank and Ken turned the wheel to the right to avoid going over, but it was no use. The car tipped over the bank, rolled twice, smashing through the ice. On its third rotation, we found ourselves under the water.

Everything was happening so fast. The back windshield had blown out on the first roll, causing the car to quickly submerge. The world was upside-down, with the roof of the car sinking quickly into the frigid water. The front of the vehicle faced upstream, the headlights still on and momentarily illuminating the water through the hole that used to be the windshield. The six of us were still in the car and it was rapidly filling up.

I was situated in the rear, driver's side seat of the car. I reached for the back window area and pulled myself out of the car. Before I could get free, the trunk pushed me to the bottom of the river, trapping me. As the current made the front end of the car go down, I reached for the back bumper and pulled myself clear of the car. I swam to the surface, then over to the shore where the car had rolled into the river. The winter sky was clear and I could see the surface of the water, but no vehicle. At some point, the electrical system had shorted, killing the headlights.

I started panicking. No one else has come to the surface. I didn't know if I should jump back in and try to save my friends or try to find help. As I was debating this, I suddenly saw someone and started yelling at him, "swim this way!" As he got close, I could see that it was my brother Ken. I helped him onto the shore just as another person surfaced. Again I yelled, "this way!" Ken and I helped him onto the shore; it was Clim Anthony.

A minute or two went by, then we saw another person appear. All three of us started yelling at them so they knew which direction to head. When we pulled him out of the water, it is Alex Woykin. We waited anxiously for Larry and Jerry, but they weren't coming out of the water. Time seemed to run too fast or too slow. Five minutes had passed since I had reached the shore. *I know I can hold my breath three or four minutes max,* I thought to myself, weighing my options. We were wet, freezing, upset, and probably suffering from shock. Seven minutes had elapsed, when I decided that there wasn't anything we could do and needed to run for help.

My wet clothes had already started to harden with ice. Time wasn't on our side. I turned to the three survivors. "Let's go!" I yelled.

"What about Larry and Jerry?" someone asked.

"It's been about ten minutes, they are not going to make it out!" No one argued with me. They knew we had to act.

We helped each other to the road, knowing that the Pepin's house was three hundred yards up the road.

Our teeth chattering, and our energy sapped, we barely made it to their house. When we finally got to their door, all four of us knocked as loud as we could. They let us in and asked what happened. I told them to call the RCMP, that we needed help now, and Larry and Jerry were still in the river. They dialled immediately and proceeded to get us towels and blankets to warm us up.

The police arrived at the scene, and searched for Larry and Jerry, who still hadn't surfaced. Another policeman drove us all home. Without waiting for confirmation, I knew I had lost two of my friends that night. When I got home, I phoned my boss and told him I wouldn't be coming to work the next day.

Later, my brother Ken explained what he had gone through to get out of the vehicle. He said he tried smashing the driver's side window, but it wouldn't break. Somehow he found a way out of the car. He couldn't remember if it was through the front or rear windshield, but suddenly he was breathing the cold air.

The next time I talked to Alex, he admitted remembering swimming under the ice and not being able to break through. He realized he had been going the wrong direction and swam back toward where he thought we had gone in and found the opening in the ice. Somehow that moment of clarity had broken through his fear and panic.

Shock is a funny thing. Some things you don't remember what happens until it's all over. If you'd asked me immediately following the accident what had happened, I wouldn't have been able to tell you. Sometime later, the clear memory of the trunk pinning me to the bottom of the river came back to me. I distinctly remembered thinking that I was wasn't going to make it out, that I was going to die down there, but somehow I had escaped death again.

That car rolled exactly between two trees and into the river. Ten feet in either direction and they would have stopped the car, but we shot right through the centre. To this day I ask myself, *why did the car jump out of the ruts and go in the direction of those two trees?* People discuss the concept of fate, of having a timeline, and when your time is up, it was meant to be. It may not have been my time to go then, but what about Jerry and Larry? They couldn't swim, so the cards were stacked against them. If they had known, would it have made a difference?

Following the accident, another memory came back to me. A few days before we plunged into that river, I had one of my prophetic dreams about Larry dying. By the time we'd gotten in that truck, I had forgotten about it. In the dream, I saw Larry in a coffin. His uncle placed his hand on Larry's chest and said goodbye. I was also standing there, saying my goodbyes to my friend.

When I woke up from my dream, it seemed so real, I asked myself, *will this happen? Where and when will this happen? Am I supposed to warn Larry?* As I always do, I filed it away and told myself it was just a dream. After the accident I wondered, *did I actually see a moment from the future?*

It's also possible that I wasn't the only one who'd had a premonition about that night. When I think back on the series of events, I remember how insistent Larry was that we come along. Both Alex and I had the opportunity to leave, but there was something in his eyes that made us stay. It's possible that if Alex or myself had backed out, more may have died in that river.

CHAPTER SIX

THE DISAPPEARING ROAD

Out one night with friends, I was driving around with Norman Ball and his girlfriend, Peggy Dow. We were driving Peggy's friend, Musky, home to Christina Lake. We were all laughing and reminiscing; I was sitting in the back on the right side of the car.

As you pass Boothman Ranch, the road curves to the right, leading into a three-quarter mile straight-stretch, before it turns left and goes up a hill. Just as we got to the bottom of the hill, we noticed a brand new road going to the left. Norman looked over his shoulder at me and said, "I've never seen this road before." The three of us agreed with him.

Norman suddenly turned toward the road, and something in my head started to scream that it wasn't a good idea. I gripped the front seat and yelled as loud as I could at Norman to stop. We had gone a hundred yards down the mystery road, dirt flying up from our tires and creating a cloud of dust. Norman glanced back at me with a smile on his face, thinking I was joking around. He quickly realized the severity of my grave concerns, and his smile faded. After a moment, he said, "I'll turn around."

"Don't even bother," I urged. "Just back up." Something in my voice had Norman shifting into reverse and punching the pedal until we were back on the main road. As the dust settled, all four of us looked through the windshield. The road was gone. It had simply vanished. Even our tire tracks ceased to indicate that we'd turned down the non-existent path. All four of us started to talk at the same time. "Oh, come on now!" "We saw it, it was just there!" "Where did it go?"

When none of us could offer a believable explanation, we decided to take Peggy's friend home and drive back to Grand Forks. As soon as Musky was out of the car, the three of stopped talking. The drive back to my house was in complete silence.

A few days later, Norman came to me, white as a sheet. He told me that earlier that day he was driving to Christina Lake. It had been stormy on the horizon, the dark clouds hanging low in the sky. He was traveling along the same route, when he recognized the spot where we had turned in. He slowed, hoping to see an opening in the trees, perhaps lay to rest the mystery of the road due to an optical illusion caused by the forest. His car had almost come to a stop in the exact same spot when a bolt of lightning hit the back of the car, scaring the hell out of him. He punched the gas and sped back home as quick as he could. At first, I thought he was trying to get a rise out of me, but like that night, I saw something in his eyes that made me believe him.

Since then, every time I drive past that point in the road going to Christina Lake, I wonder if we also would have disappeared, had we traveled any farther down the road that night. I still wonder, *where did it come from, and where did it disappear to after we were on it?*

It's been many decades, and I'm still waiting for an answer.

CHAPTER SEVEN

WORK AND DREAMS

From the time I was a kid I was taught that it was my responsibility to do chores, to work, and contribute to the family. It's not surprising that early in my life I established myself in the workforce, and continued to succeed. I went to work for another farmer in Grand Forks and eventually earned enough to buy my own tractor, a 1950 Ferguson two-plow. I started doing custom work: plowing, disking, and harrowing. I had created a steady cash flow and was getting paid decent wages, so my Dad and I bought a brand new three-plow tractor, a Massey Ferguson with a front end loader, a three-point hitch-slide delivery rake, and a Massey Ferguson hay baler with its own sixteen horse-power motor. It was pretty exciting for a guy my age to be able to attain so many practical toys that early in my life.

We were able to do custom haying, which made enough extra money for our household. We both wanted to make life easier for my mother, so we bought new appliances and fixed up the house to make it more livable. I still had my jobs with the farmers, changing one-hundred fifty sprinklers at a rate of three cents per sprinkler. I would change them morning and night, seven days a week. Despite making three cents per, which a kid of the same age today would balk at, I was living the good life. I was bailing from 8:00 am to 4:00 pm then servicing the sprinklers after that, doing a great business, and smiling when I went to bed.

I was out baling hay above Spencer's Hill one afternoon. I had the Ford 8N tractor going fifteen miles per hour as I came down the hill. I thought if I put the tractor into neutral, I could go down the hill faster, and make it home a little quicker. The hill was two-thirds of a mile long, and I was going faster than I felt comfortable, so I stepped on the brake only to find the tractor and the baler jack-knifing. At that speed, the brake wasn't going to help me, so I held off. The steering arms started wobbling and I had to push on them with my feet to keep them steady. I was passing cars at about 50 or 60 mph. I'm not sure how, but I made it to the bottom, unscathed and with the tractor intact. It was a hell of a ride, but reaffirmed the old saying about being in a rush.

My vivid dreams had become a regular part of my life. I was having them every night, and had come to expect them as I fell asleep. I started to experience more out-of-body journeys, in which I would drift out of my sleeping body and travel around to different places. I still wasn't sure what it was, and wondered if other people had the same experience. I didn't want to ask anyone and have them think I was crazy, so I just kept it to myself and coped with it as best I could.

One night, during one of my dreams, I woke up choking. A 50 year-old man with a balding head was on my chest. I crossed my hands and pushed at his chest, trying to knock him off of me. He let go and disappeared into the dark. As I lay there, breathing deeply, I came to the conclusion that, as real as it felt, it had been a dream. It was hard to shake the feeling that the man had been in my room. I didn't sleep any more that night, as I analyzed everything around me. I knew I had left no doors open to my room. I knew that he couldn't have come in through the window. It had to have been a dream!

The next morning, I went into the bathroom and looked at myself in the mirror. Around my neck were bruises, exactly where the man had held me in my dream. To this day, I have no explanation for what could've caused it. If there was a man, where did he go? Why did I picture him so vividly? And if I did it to myself, why? Could I have died that night? I hoped I'd never have to go through something like it again. Turns out I would...

In 1972 I was working out of town planting trees and living in a camp. One night I was woken up by a man on my chest choking me. This appeared to be the same man I had encountered previously. I didn't know why he was there, or where he came from.

Once again, I crossed my hands across my chest and pushed. I was running out of air so I gave another push, and again this apparition disappeared into the night. Thoughts careened around in my head. *Where did he come from? Why was he attacking me? How did he get here?*

I began to wonder, *when I dream, do I open a doorway that allows him in? If so, from where?*

Even though it was over, I felt as though I had another close brush with death. I didn't know if I was seeing a premonition of my own death or if I had called this being into existence. I had a lot of questions, but no answers.

CHAPTER EIGHT

SAND CREEK

Hunting and fishing have always been a huge part of our lives; we lived off the land. The animals on the farm, the chickens, the gardens, hunting wild game, and fishing were all routine at the Ritco home.

As any sixteen year-old in that part of the world, I had my hunting license. As we did every year, Dad and I were going up to Sand Creek; he had his favourite spots to hunt and fish, and I had mine. We always had a contingency plan in place in case something happened in the bush. That day, we decided we would meet at the truck after four hours, no exceptions.

I checked my watch and headed down the open hill into the bottom of a draw, where it was thick with brush and deer liked to graze. I stopped in the middle of the draw and looked back up at the open slope. The brush was about ten feet high and I'm only 5'6". Suddenly, I heard a rifle shot and a piece of brush ten inches to the left of my head falls. There was another shot and more brush fell. *Oh my god,* I thought, *someone is shooting at me!* It was rare, but someone could mistake you for an animal and just start shooting. I didn't know if I was going to get out of there alive.

I froze, not moving an inch. Even though everything in my body was screaming at me to hit the dirt, I didn't duck down as ten shots were fired. I finally raised my gun and fired three times in the air, hoping to alert whoever was shooting that another hunter was in the area. That person must have realized and high-tailed it out of the area because I raced up the hill hoping to find the shooter, but I didn't find anyone. Based on the amount, I knew the shooter had a rifle equipped with a ten shot clip, so it couldn't have been my dad, who's gun only held five rounds.

Only after I'd exhausted my search did I realize how close to death I'd come...again.

CHAPTER NINE

LIGHTNING STRIKES

One of my chores on our family farm was to milk the cow. When I was almost seventeen years old, as usual after dinner, I went out to the barn and opened the door. I let the cow into its stall and gave her grain and alfalfa hay.

I looked down and saw that there was three inches of milk in the pail. All of a sudden a bolt of lightning hit between the cow and me. The cow was slammed into the wall and I was thrown ten feet into the opposite wall. The milk pail went flying, spraying milk all over the place.

I stood up and immediately looked at the cow, hoping she was okay. She looked at me and I couldn't help but think, *she thinks it was me who slammed her into the wall!* She confirmed my suspicions by suddenly letting out a loud bellow! I didn't have time to feel guilty, I was still reeling about the fact that neither of us had been killed!

I went into the house and told my mom and my brother Ken what had happened. My mom checked to make sure I didn't have any burns on me, and Ken couldn't help but laugh at the milk dripping from me.

It ended up being a pretty good lightning storm that night. Later, Ken decided to get a glass of water. Not realizing there was any danger, Ken grabbed a glass out of the cupboard and turned on the tap. Flames came shooting out of the tap, scaring the hell out of all of us. Like my earlier incident, Ken was unharmed, but we sure learned to respect Mother Nature when she's in a mood.

CHAPTER TEN

ZIBBIN CON. LTD.

By my late teens, I had found a job working for a local logging company, Zibbin Con. Ltd., driving a 540 John Deer Skidder.

Up in the dense forests of the mountain the ground is steep, including the logging roads. I was going down a hill, the skidder moving pretty fast, when the skidder did a complete somersault and landed on its roof one trail below. Somehow I managed to stay in the vehicle without getting hurt.

A few days later, I had one of my dreams. In it I was flying through the air in a vehicle I didn't recognize. It had a half-circle steering wheel, but I couldn't see any other part of the vehicle. When I awoke, I tried to analyze the dream, thinking that I was misremembering details from my earlier accident. I distinctly remembered the details of the vehicle being different, and wondered if this was a portent of things to come.

A couple of days after that, Zibbin bought a brand new 404 Timber Jack Skidder. Since I had experience, the foreman asked me to drive it. We were logging on Gable Mountain, where the ground was so steep that my co-worker Paul and I had to winch our machines through the timber at the edge of the block to get to the top.

I start down the mountain, stopping to hook the first tree with a choker and so on down the mountain. Soon, there are no more trees at the top, the trees had kept the skidder from flipping end over end. I am slowly creeping down the mountain, taking my time, but due to the steep grade, the skidder slides sideways, and goes onto two wheels, it's going to roll. I hold onto the steering wheel, and try to climb out, I am between the two wheels in the air, there is not enough room to jump clear, the skidder tips more. I know, if I am caught between the wheels when it rolls, the skidder will roll on top of me and I will be killed!

I make a decision, I get back inside the skidder, I hear the D.G. Cat coming towards me. The choker man yells out, "we'll pull you back onto your wheels!" But, the skidder is now slowly tipping more, my only chance is to try and turn downhill. I put the skidder into first gear, the DG Cat is not going to get there in time, I know that, I have to come up with something else.

So I decided to floor it and turn downhill, I brace my feet on the dashboard, too late! The skidder is sliding down the mountain on its roof. Not only are we sliding down the mountain, the skidder, hits a stump, I am now airborne, it does one somersault, it now hits the ground and bounces back into the air.

As I am in the air, I realize, this is just like my dream, the half circle steering wheel, I am just flying! The skidder rolls a couple of times, I am hanging on for dear life, it lands on its wheels and is one-inch-thick steel inward by three to four inches. Wow! I am still alive, I almost got killed!

I drove the skidder to the landing and told my boss what had happened, he told me if I had rolled the skidder, I wouldn't be there telling him about it. Blood is pouring down over my left eye. After work, back in Grand Forks, the doctor put six stitches in the cut, I went back to work the next day, but this time, the boss said to put chains on the skidder, apparently he found out that I did in fact roll the skidder and was there to tell him. I carried on working the same slope until Paul and I had all the trees skidded in.

CHAPTER ELEVEN

IN THE TRUNK

Bernie and I are old friends. We have a tendency to get into things together, but it's always a good laugh and a fun time. We were out one night having a few beers with another friend, Gordy. Now Gordy has a few problems, he's mentally challenged and sometimes he gets carried away.

After a few beers, Gordy said he was losing it. He turned to Bernie, who was driving at the time, and demanded to be put in the trunk of the car. Bernie, being a good friend and knowing how Gordy would get, stopped the car and opened the trunk. It was no surprise that Gordy got out and climbed in.

As Gordy was climbing in, Bernie looked at the three things now in the trunk: a bale of hay, a can of gas, and Gordy. "Don't you smoke in there," Bernie said. Gordy smiled and promised not to.

We continued driving around town, when a local Mountie turned on his lights and pulled us over. "Open the trunk," he said, "I want to see if you have any beer." Bernie complied and opened it. The police officer looked and saw Gordy smiling up at him. You would think the officer would have thrown the book at us for having someone locked in the trunk of the car, but he said nothing, slammed the trunk and walked back to the window.

"Get the hell out of town," he ordered and turned back to his cruiser. Bernie and I just looked at each other and we left as fast as we could.

Two hours later, Gordy finally settled down, so we let him back in the car and carried on with our typical night on the town in Grand Forks.

CHAPTER TWELVE

BEAR-HUNTING SEASON

Summer was over and the fall colours had taken over, which meant that hunting season was open. My friend Stanley came to my house and told me he wanted to go to the Christina Lake City Dump to shoot a bear. *Why not,* I thought. So we called up our friend Doug to come as well.

We got out to the dump and Stan immediately saw a bear up in one of the trees lining the dump. Without waiting for the perfect moment, he raised his rifle, aimed, and shot at the giant animal. His first shot wounded the bear, which is not a good thing when you don't have a lot of shells. When he fired the last bullet, the bear fell out of the tree, its 400 pound frame shuddering the ground. The bear started pulling up and ripping brush out of the dirt as it bled out. Because of the ruckus, more bears showed up, which we took as an indication to get out of there as fast as we could. We left the wounded bear and headed back into town.

The next day, Stanley asked me to go bear hunting again. "No," I replied. "I'm not a bear hunter. I had enough yesterday, thank you." As a compromise, we decided to go grouse hunting instead. We went up above Grand Forks, and Stanley brought his dog, Cassidy. We weren't there for very long before a grouse flew up out of a bush and I shot it. My celebration was short-lived since the brush was so thick I couldn't find where the body landed. Eventually, I grew tired of looking for it and went back to my spot just as another grouse took flight. I shot it and watched where it fell, not thinking to reload my shotgun.

I was looking for the second grouse, going through the bush in a straight line from where I fired. When I found the grouse, I put my shotgun on the ground. I picked up the dead bird with my right hand and turned to my left to pick up my shotgun. Just as I was turning back I realized there was a hole in the ground with a big black bear looking at me and growling. The bear was not happy to see me, and I wasn't too thrilled about it either. His head was 18 inches across, his mouth was open, and he was baring his teeth, each one at least three inches long. I slowly stood, turned, and ran!

That bear was out of that hole with surprising speed and was right behind me. My adrenaline kicked in; I was running so fast my legs felt like they were just a blur. I yelled out to Stanley, warning him that there was a bear on my heels. He let Cassidy off her leash and she ran straight for me before quickly passing me as she intercepted the bear. I could hear them behind me, growling at each other. The bear eventually wandered away. I took my grouse and headed home.

Stanley showed up the next day and asked me if I wanted to go hunting again. "No thanks," I replied. "I almost got killed yesterday. I don't think I want to go hunting with you again."

CHAPTER THIRTEEN

FALLING AND FLYING

In 1968, I decided to try my luck in another town, city, or province...it didn't matter where. My brother-in-law Veral was living in Calgary, and he helped me get a job as a labourer on a highrise project. Veral gave me a job jackhammering the elevator shaft. I was told I had to make it straight so the elevator could work inside of it. It had to be kept perfect for all twenty-two floors, which I succeeded in completing.

My next job was to work with another guy who was twenty years older than me. Our job was to start at the uppermost floor and, as each new floor was being completed, go around the exterior of the building on the scaffolding that was attached to fly forms. We had a hydraulic cable stressing machine that lightened the cables that ran across each floor. This was a new design made for earthquake and wind movement stability. There were two sets of fly forms, one for the top floor and one for the floor below. The carpenters would get the crane to lift the forms to the next floor up as each was completed.

We had just completed stressing the cables going around the floor just below the top. We reached the second floor with the 60 pound stressing machine, and agreed that we'd successfully completed another floor. We both looked back to where we just were and saw that all the fly forms were gone. The crane had just laid rebar on the top floor, which caused a slight movement in the building, and the forms we were just standing on had fallen twenty-two floors. We could have been killed! The foreman reminded the carpenters not to move the forms until we had finished stressing, which should have been mentioned before the lives of two employees were put in danger.

Spring was coming and I had enough of working in Alberta, so I decided it was time to go home to Grand Forks. I immediately arranged for a plane ticket from Calgary to Castlegar, called my Dad, and he told me he and my brothers would pick me up upon my arrival. I was glad to be going home.

The day of the flight was a good day. Everything was in order as I headed out to the airport. After a short wait, I boarded the plane, feeling that all was well. The plane took off and we were flying over the mountains, between B.C. and Alberta, when the plane started to become choppy, feeling like it could drop at any moment. The flight attendant told us it was probably from an air pocket. I didn't need a scientific explanation to know that I wasn't enjoying the flight very much.

At one point, I looked out the window and saw the motor on my side had stopped. *Well isn't that great,* I think, *we are now going for one hell of a ride.* The attendant could barely walk down the aisle, hanging onto seats to steady herself. As she went past me, I said, "did you notice that this engine is not working?"

"Yes," she replied. At that moment, the captain then announced, "we have one engine down." *At least they know,* I thought.

We were almost over Castlegar and the wind was extremely strong. The captain came over the speaker and announced, "everybody get your crash pillows out and buckle up! We have one chance to land this plane, I'm going to go into a dive at the end of the runway to land."

I looked out the window and yes, we were in a dive. The captain pulled the plane up and landed the plane safely. Everybody thanked him as we disembarked. If it wasn't for his skill and determination, we all would have died. I'm sure more than one of us kissed the ground when we got off.

CHAPTER FOURTEEN

CABBAGE AND ELECTRICITY

The fall of 1970 saw my friend Chuck Thomas and I flat broke. We had no money to buy beer, so we decided to go to the Phoenix Mine Dump Site, as we did on occasion. There was always a chance to find something out there, maybe a few batteries we could sell for beer money. So we took off and drove to the dump.

When we arrived at the dump, the sun had gone down, and the site was dark. We turned the car around and backed up to where we saw an old radiator. Chuck opened the trunk, we picked up the 200 pound radiator and flop it into the trunk. It bears mentioning here that back in 1970, our hair was slicked back with Brylcreem, not the long, free-flowing style that became popular a few years later.

We started smelling rotten cabbage and mine and Chuck's hair felt like it was electrified and sticking out in every direction. We were both scared, knowing something wasn't right. We got in the car and moved twenty feet when something jumped onto the trunk. It started scratching the back of the car, which was dragging on the ground. Chuck drove down the narrow old road, the wind buffeting the vehicle. All of a sudden whatever had jumped on the car, fell off. We didn't have a flashlight, and neither of us wanted to get out to investigate, so we couldn't identify it.

The radiator turned out to be made of steel and had no value, so we couldn't buy beer that night. We decided to go back there the next day. This time I took my 303 with two clips of 220 grain bullets, and my pump action shotgun. Chuck brought his rifle. We also remembered to bring flashlights, but when we arrived and went into the old mine shafts, we found nothing.

The next day, on a bluff two miles away, I found what looked like a four-inch-wide heel print on the edge of a molehill.

When the weekend arrived, my brother Ken and his friend Dean Cown drove up to the old TV transmitter with their girlfriends. Ken and his girlfriend started a fire a hundred feet away from Dean and his girlfriend. They were enjoying the evening when suddenly their hair stood up and they smelled rotten cabbage. Later, Ken told me that a nine-foot, hairy, repulsive Sasquatch walked up to Ken's fire, reached up and ripped two three-inch fir branches off the tree. Ken, Dean, and their girlfriends ran to the car, got in, and got the hell out of there.

Hearing the story, we decided to go back up there the next morning. Ken and Dean brought their rifles, and my brothers Dan and Dale decided to come along, also armed with their hunting rifles. I brought my camera, my rifle, and my twelve gauge. We only wanted pictures but, just in case, we were ready to protect ourselves. We headed up there and, sure enough, the branches of the fir tree were freshly broken off, right by the fire from the night before.

We all looked for tracks, but the needles and grass had covered the ground. Some reading this chapter will scoff, and there are certainly a fair share of skeptics, but there's also a lot of believers out there. No one knows for sure, but whatever was running around the Phoenix Dump and at the old TV Transmitter wasn't anything familiar to us, and we have lived in the area our entire lives.

Who knows what's possible? Quite often above the mountains in Grand Forks, you can see lights in the sky. Could there be other unexplainable phenomenon around this area?

CHAPTER FIFTEEN

KEN AND RON VS. THE FISH

My brother, Ken, and I liked to go fishing each spring when the river main channel opened. There would still be ice on the lakes and rivers, and in 1970 we decided to go fishing on Christina Lake, which was one of our favourite spots. The ice was ten inches thick, and we took out a sled that was packed with fishing gear and food. We got set up to wait for the fish with full intentions of taking some home for dinner.

My dad, who had been fishing those lakes for years, had found a new spot to fish for burbot and inland cod. Ken and I started along the east side of the lake, then Indian Head Rock, then a few more spots before we got to the cedar tree, dad's new spot. We decided we would try there for a while to see what happened. It could be good fishing; we wouldn't know until we tried.

Ken was fishing a hundred fifty feet from the shore, but I stuck closer to it. I'd drilled an air hole ten inches across. I dropped my line down where the depth was forty feet. We were using hand lines wrapped on a 16-inch-long V-Cut Board, and it wasn't long before I had a bite. I knew right away that the fish was big; it wouldn't stop taking the line, just kept pulling more and more.

I yelled at Ken to come over and help me. He was facing away when I yelled at him again. I could hear him laugh, thinking I was just pulling his leg and trying to distract him, so I'd land the first one. I yelled, "Ken, look at my line!" Something in my voice made him turn. Seeing the line, he abandoned his line and ran over.

"Holy shit!" he exclaimed as he grabbed the line and we started pulling the fish up together. We predicted that this could be larger than most we had caught out there. Ken said, "what if this is like a Loch Ness Monster?"

"Then we'll pull it up and kill it," I replied. He laughed as we continued to pull the ⅛" thick leader line. The thing was giving us a run for our money; we weren't even sure what the hell we had caught on our line.

Finally, we pulled it up on the ice, whatever it was. We could tell it was big but we couldn't see a head or tail, only a large, dark, green shape. Ken grabbed the gaff and pinned the thing, making sure it couldn't turn around and get one of us. He pulled a two-inch piece from it and then the hook came out. The fish slipped back into the water and was gone. We laughed and agreed that whatever it had been, it was big.

That wasn't the first time I had seen some odd creature out at the lake. My dad and I had hooked something large ten years earlier up at the lake past Deer Point, but it got off the hook and we never saw it, so I wasn't able to compare it to what Ken and I pulled out of the lake that day.

My brother Dale and my dad told us that they also hooked something huge out at the lake one time, but it also took off so they weren't able to describe what it was they had caught out there. To this day, I still can't swim in Christina Lake.

If Ken and I could easily pull 200 pounds each, that fish or whatever it was, had been enormous. I can say, no one has caught that fish, to date.

One spring, Ken and I went down to the river to the old Collin's Ranch. We were excited about going out on the lake and doing some fishing. There was a pumphouse on the west side of the farm, right by a bay area. That spring there was a 10 x 20 foot piece of ice at the shore, attached to a 40-foot-wide and 60-foot-long piece of ice jutting out into the river.

We carefully crept across the narrow piece of ice and got onto the larger attached piece. Someone had been fishing there before us and we could see a few old holes left in the ice. We both took advantage of the already-drilled holes and dropped our lines in. There was only four feet of water and the ice was ten inches thick.

It wasn't long before Ken jerked his line and said, "I got a bite." I was also getting a few bites. A couple minutes went by, I looked down into the water and could see the bottom.

I turned to my brother. "Ken, look down in the hole."

"The ice is moving," he responded. By the time we noticed, the piece of ice had separated from the shore. We really did not want to swim twenty feet in the cold water to make it back to shore. Regardless, we were heading down the river whether we liked it or not.

Ken figured he could resolve the situation by simply chopping the front of the ice into the shape of a boat. He took his axe and started hacking at the ice. As Ken was chopping away, I said, "Ken, turn around."

He had been chopping so effectively, he separated himself from the piece of ice I was standing on. He now found himself on a separate piece of ice that had broken off. Without thinking, he quickly ran and jumped onto the piece I was on, however he was in such a rush to get off the drifting section, he left his axe and fishing rod, which continued floating down the river ahead of us.

Ahead of us we saw a sharp bend to the right. As we approached the corner, the piece of ice ran right up onto shore. We figured that was our chance to jump off our makeshift vessel, but the back of the ice went under the water and we began slipping around. Suddenly the whole piece of ice shattered like glass, forcing us to jump from piece to piece to prevent us from going in the water. We managed to both wind up on a 12 x 18 foot piece of ice.

At this point I noticed that my fishing rod and axe were also gone! Being the kind of people who take things in stride, Ken and I just started laughing. We figured we had never traveled down the river on a piece of ice before, and here we were floating along with the current, we might as well just enjoy the ride.

Continuing along, we noticed a man to our right on the shore watching us. He called out, "you guys are crazy!" *He's right,* I thought, *who goes floating down the river on a chunk of ice in the spring?* We couldn't help but laugh. We floated along for half a mile, watching and hoping for a chance to get off the ice floe as soon as possible.

Up ahead, we saw there was another bend in the river turning left. As I was thinking, *it must be our lucky day*, the piece of ice hit the shore. Ken and I simply stepped onto shore, laughing. We walked the three miles home and dad drove us back so we could get our car. Adventure had found us again and, because of our perspective, we were able to enjoy the fun.

CHAPTER SIXTEEN

SONGS

I have shared many experiences of my life up to this point. It is probably obvious that I have a great imagination, and a curiosity for life. Throughout my life, I've written poems and songs about the things I observed and experienced.

In 1976, I sent my songs to a producer in Nashville. Here's his response:

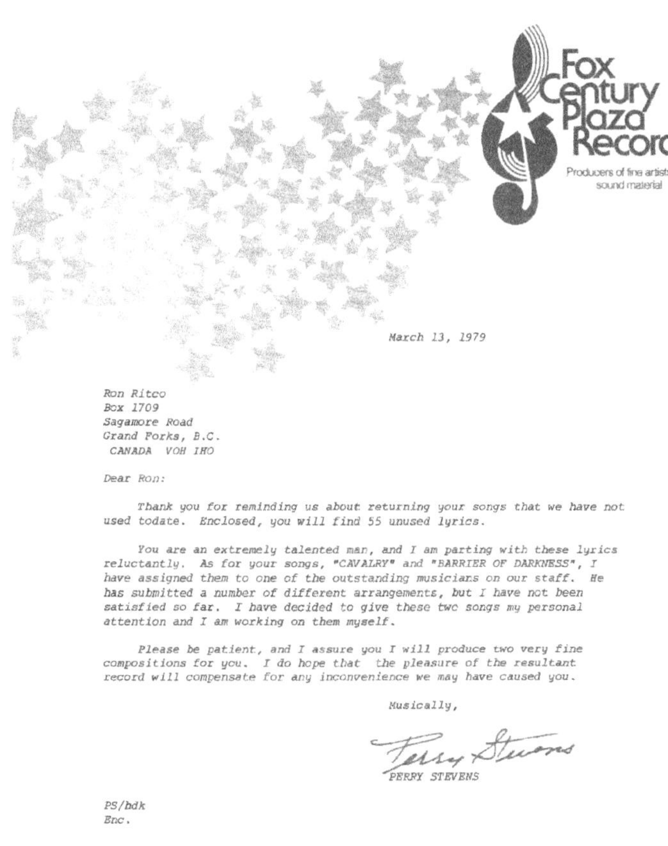

Fox Century Plaza Records

Producers of fine artists and sound material

March 13, 1979

Ron Ritco
Box 1709
Sagamore Road
Grand Forks, B.C.
CANADA VOH IHO

Dear Ron:

Thank you for reminding us about returning your songs that we have not used todate. Enclosed, you will find 55 unused lyrics.

You are an extremely talented man, and I am parting with these lyrics reluctantly. As for your songs, "CAVALRY" and "BARRIER OF DARKNESS", I have assigned them to one of the outstanding musicians on our staff. He has submitted a number of different arrangements, but I have not been satisfied so far. I have decided to give these two songs my personal attention and I am working on them myself.

Please be patient, and I assure you I will produce two very fine compositions for you. I do hope that the pleasure of the resultant record will compensate for any inconvenience we may have caused you.

Musically,

Perry Stevens

PERRY STEVENS

PS/bdk
Enc.

1920 Chestnut Street, Suite 901 • Philadelphia, Pa. 19103 • (215) 567-7718

Even though I intended for my songs to be sung by other artists, none ever made the charts, but I enjoyed the adventure and still hope one day that someone will see the potential and bring my words to life.

WVT-19M
POWER OF LOVE BY JOHN PATRICK
THE POW-ER OF LOVE HURTS DEEP IN-SIDE,
WHEN YOUR HEART BE-GINS TO CRY. IT WAS BROKEN BY AN
EV-IL GUY; BA-BY, YOU'RE GONNA HAVE TO SAY GOOD-
BYE___ YOU TRY TO CON-TROL IT AS YOU WEEP, BUT THE
POW-ER OF LOVE HURTS, OH, SO DEEP! WHEN YOUR HEART BE-
GINS TO CRY; IT WAS BRO-KEN BY AN EV-IL
GUY___ WHAT WAS MEANT TO BE, WILL SURE-LY
COME___ BUT SOON-ER OR LA-TER,
THERE WILL BE AN-OTH-ER LOVE___ OH, THE
POW-ER OF LOVE HURTS DEEP IN-SIDE; OH, THE
POW-ER OF LOVE HURTS DEEP IN-SIDE___
TALENT SEARCHERS Of Hollywood
311 Yucca Ave., Hollywood, California 90028 PRESENT THIS COMPOSITION FOR YOUR CONSIDERATION.

WVT-18M
TR.14
PRAIRIE
BY JOHN PATRICK
WE SAVED OUR NICKLES, SAVED OUR DIMES, TO
GO OUT WEST IN THE SUMMERTIME; AND BUILT OUR CABIN
OUT OF ROCK AND STONE, ON THE PRAIRIE LAND WE
OWNED ___ WIN-TER CAME SO HARD AND STRONG; THE
PRAIRIE WIND WOULD BLOW A - LONG; SPRING TIME CAME AND YOU
GAVE ME A SON, THERE WAS MORE BETWEEN US THAN JUST
LOVE ___ I PLANT-ED CROPS AND BY AND BY, THE
WHEAT AND RYE GREW HIGH; THEN THE FALLTIME CAME, THE
CROPS WERE RIPE; YOU AND I WOULD WORK ALL NIGHT ___ AND
BY AND BY, THE WHEAT AND RYE, GREW
HIGH ON THE PRAIRIE SIDE ___ THEN TWO YEARS LATER WE HAD
TWO MORE SONS, AND OUR DREAMS CAME TRUE ON THE
PRAIR-IE ___ BY AND BY ON THE PRAIRIE SIDE ___ FADE
TALENT SEARCHERS
of Hollywood
6311 Yucca Ave., Hollywood, California 90028 PRESENT THIS COMPOSITION FOR YOUR CONSIDERATION.

<u>Captain Ace</u>- by Ron Ritco   Written on Sept. 25, 1976

A crew of Kings sailing on a ship of Queens   *Copyright, Oct. 27, 1976*

Across an ocean only made of Threes

Four mighty Jacks standing on the deck

Ordering Ten to do their very best

Nine masts are blowing in the mighty wind

Eight foot high waves are rollin in

Seven more miles of raging sea

Six more men we have lost at sea

Five days of travel are near it s end

Four more hours the Captains wheel will last

But only on a sea of Threes

Can a ship with Two sides ever be

A crew of Kings sailing on a ship of Queens

Across an ocean only made of Threes

Four mighty Jacks standing on the deck

Ordering Ten to their very best

Nine masts are blowing in the mighty winds

Eight foot high waves are rollin in

Seven more miles of raging sea

Six more men we have lost at sea

Five days of travel are near its end

Four more hours the Captains wheel will last

But only on a sea of Threes

Can a ship with Two sides ever be

One is the Captain, The Captain of the deck

And all alone he can beat the rest. He can beat the rest!!!

"ASTRAL WOMAN"
WORDS + MUSIC BY_
RON RITCO
MOD.
I TOOK A LA_DY FROM A CRYSTAL SEA. I SET HER FREE
SO THAT SHE COULD BE. I SHOWED HER NIGHT, I
SHOWED HER DAY. I SHOWED HER THE WORLD ON A SUN_NY DAY_
I TOLD HER THAT THE EARTH WAS THE SON OF THE
SUN. THE EARTH WAS THE SUN OF LOVE. THE
MOON WAS A LA_DY_. FILLED WITH LOVE AND SHE
SHONE HER LOVE ON EARTH EV'RY NIGHT
I TOLD HER THAT THE STARS THAT FILLED THE SKIES WERE
HEA_VEN'S SOLD_IERS AND THEY NEV_ER DIE_ I
Fox Century Plaza Records

KILL ME IF YOU CAN

Fox Century Plaza Records

WM21T
TR.14
SOUL BY RONALD RITCO
8 BAR INTRO
PEOPLE ARE COLORED, MAN-Y A SHADE; BUT
IN-SIDE THEIR SOULS, ALL ARE THE SAME. WE'RE
ALL ON THIS EARTH FOR A PURPOSE IT SEEMS, AND
WHEN OUR JOB IS DONE, WE'LL SURELY LEAVE. I'M OLD AND TIRED,
MY JOB IS DONE; I'LL BE LEAVING SOON, I
GIVE YOU MY LOVE. WHEN I LAY DOWN AND I DIE, DON'T
CRY FOR ME, HERE'S WHY—— EV-'RY-BOD-Y'S SOUL IS
YOUNG AND A-LIVE, AND WHEN YOUR BOD-Y DIES, IT FLIES!
HEAVEN'S DOOR, I WILL SEE IT SOON, I KNOW IT'S TRUE, MY BE-
LIEFS ARE TRUE. OH, EV-'RY- BOD-Y'S SOUL; OH, EV-'RY-
BOD-Y'S SOUL; OH, EV-'RY- BOD-Y'S SOUL
WILL SOON COME HOME——
TALENT SEARCHERS Of Hollywood
6311 Yucca Ave., Hollywood, California 90028 PRESENT THIS COMPOSITION FOR YOUR CONSIDERATION.

RON RITCO
"BARRIER OF DARKNESS"
SLOW
BREAK THRU THE BAR-RI-ER OF DARK-NESS
I WANT TO SEE THE LIGHT OF THE DAY
THERE IS DARK-NESS IN MY LIFE COME CLOSER
YOU CAN SHOW ME THE WAY BREAK THRU THE
BAR-RI-ER OF DARK-NESS I WANT TO SEE THE
LIGHT OF DAY I'VE TRAVELED FAR BUT
I'M NOT GET-TING A-NY CLOSER CAN YOU SHOW ME THE WAY
CAN YOU SHOW ME THE WAY
REPEAT MY LIFE IS DARK-NESS COME SHOW ME
Fox Century Plaza Records

Fox Century Plaza Records

Music-City Entertainer Page 15

New Faces

Being a logger in the wilds of British Columbia has certainly brought out the talents in Ron Ritco. The 26 year old songwriter has a song called, "Lovin'" that has caught the attention of a few artist in music city and hopefully is on its way to being recorded.

Ron Ritco

CHAPTER SEVENTEEN

LIME CREEK LOGGING

Once again I was working for another logging company, Lime Creek Logging, falling and bucking trees.

Paul Andreas, a friend of mine, worked with me on the same site. We would fall a tree and then "limb it." One tree, we cut at the forty-nine foot mark. Just as I finished the cut, all of a sudden everything began to slide. I ran on the log and jumped into the edge of the block, while everything slid down the seventy-five foot decline of the mountain. There's no feeling like the ground beneath your feet moving away from you.

Paul and I continued to work, finishing the falling and bucking of the block. Hank McInnes, another worker on the site, asked me if I would hook up the chokers for him. I said yes, as I had no trees lined up at the moment and had the time.

As I went to work hooking up chokers, a young man started working alongside me. He and I were busy with the chokers, and every once in awhile the logs would hit the edge of the landing, or a rock would roll down. Hank, another worker, would yell "rock," giving us a warning so we could get out of the way.

Being aware of all of the hazards, we would only go so far before stopping. We were down from the high-lead yarder about 600 feet, when the butt of a tree hit the bank of the landing, loosening a rock. Whenever Hank would yell, I would look up, and this particular time I saw a round boulder ten feet in diameter coming down the mountain. It was coming right at us when it hit another rock and split in half, causing two large rocks to hurtle in our direction.

The two halves were crossing back and forth, and the young guy says, "what are we going to do?"

"Stand still!" I yelled out. We had nowhere to to run. "Wait until it's right here, then step to one side or the other!"

He didn't listen to me and started running back and forth. I was focused on the two halves coming towards me, weaving across each other's path. I watched as they collided and began moving away from each other. I was in the perfect spot, one half to my left and one half to my right. They missed me by four feet on either side.

That young fellow next to me got lucky, the two halves somehow missed him as well. I yelled up the bank, "Hank, yell little rock or big rock, next time!"

He called back, "okay Ron." Working in the bush most of my life, I've learned that it can be treacherous work at times. Hopefully no one gets hurt or killed when an accident happens, but after it occurs, you put it behind you and everyone goes back to work like nothing happened. It's a part of the job: just another day, another dollar.

CHAPTER EIGHTEEN

BEFORE MEREDITH

My strange dreams continued to be a nightly occurrence; always vivid, sometimes beautiful and inspiring, sometimes curious, and sometimes disturbing, leaving me with a feeling of helplessness to change what I had witnessed in my dream state.

One night, two and half years before I met my wife Meredith, I had one of those disturbing dreams.

In my dream, I found myself in a bedroom. I saw a lady on the left side of the bed and a man sleeping on her right. I didn't know these people and couldn't recognize my surroundings. I also noticed a crib six feet from the bed with a sleeping baby in it. Everyone was sound asleep.

I asked myself, *why am I here?* I looked over at the woman and I knew that something was terribly wrong, that the woman was in trouble. When I looked around, trying to assuage my fear, I noticed blood on the mattress. I wasn't sure what to do. Someone had to alert them that she was in trouble, and I couldn't talk to them or tell them to wake up!

What to do? I suddenly had the idea to go to the crib and poke the baby in the ribs on its exposed left side. When I did, the baby screamed out, confirming that it either felt my jab or was aware of my presence somehow. The man woke up and looked at his right hand, covered in blood. He knew right away that something was terribly wrong. He jumped out of bed, wrapped the woman in a sheet, and carried her out of the bedroom.

I awoke from my dream state, wondering what that was all about. I had no idea who these people were and why I would be seeing them in dreams. I was glad I had been able to wake that baby and let the man known he had to help the woman. I filed it away in my memories, knowing that to forget this dream would be to forget something important.

When Meredith and I met years later, one day she told me that she had hemorrhaged after having a baby and had almost bled to death, but somehow her husband had woken up when the baby cried and he had gotten her to the hospital just in time. I remembered my dream and told her what had happened. Instead of being skeptical, she immediately believed me. We knew from the day we met that we were connected, and this was just one more of those things that confirmed we were meant to be together and love one another.

CHAPTER NINETEEN

THE LOVE OF MY LIFE

As with many men, I had dated a few girls along the way, but no one that I felt a deep connection with. I craved and dreamed of meeting someone I could love and cherish, build a family, and make a life with. I asked God, *could you please let me find one woman to have and hold for the rest of my life?*

That night was one when my dreams brought me happiness and joy. I dreamt of a beautiful woman wearing a blue dress, with her hair up, and looking up at the stars. I knew it in my heart, *this is my lady, this is the one I've been searching for! Where is she? When will I meet her?*

The next night, I had the same vivid dream. Night after night, she would be in my dreams. This continued for two years. I knew she was out there somewhere and I was going to find this beautiful angel who was meant for me.

Whenever I was out around town, wherever I was, whatever I was doing, I looked constantly everywhere but could never find her.

One day, my friend Paul and I decided to go to the Yale Hotel to have a beer. We sat down at one of the tables and a barmaid who was new in town came to the table. When she asked us what we wanted, I looked up, and there she was, the beautiful lady I'd been dreaming about for two years. I was in awe and totally speechless. Paul said, "I'll have a beer."

I wanted to reply, "I want *you*. You are the woman I have been searching for!" Instead, I asked for a beer as well. "I'm Ron and this is Paul," I added.

She smiled, "my name is Meredith." My dreamgirl had finally showed up, but I wasn't sure how to get close to her, or get her to go out with me, but I was determined to figure it out.

Now that I knew where she was, I kept showing up in the bar, and after a few visits, I finally got up the courage to ask her if she would like to go for a motorcycle ride the next Saturday. She said yes! I asked where she lived and was surprised to hear that she was living with my old friends, Norman and Peggy Ball, the same people that drove to Christina Lake with me onto the road that had disappeared. I felt we already had a connection; Norman and I had been friends for a long time and I knew Meredith's sister Peggy as well.

I started thinking she wouldn't even show up to meet with me, so I didn't show up on Saturday. I thought she wouldn't come and convinced myself that I was just wasting my time. After chastising myself for being an idiot, I got my courage up one more time and went to the Yale to see if I could talk to her. My dream lady wasn't afraid to confront me. When I walked in, she asked "why didn't you come?"

"I didn't think you would come," I replied.

She looked at me. "I'll go for a ride *this* Saturday."

I was glad I had been given another chance, so when Saturday arrived, I actually showed up, and away we went. We took the motorcycle to go swimming. I wanted the chance to spend time with her, talk to her, and get to know this woman I had been seeing in my dreams for two years. I was hoping we would have a nice, cozy, place by the lake to swim, talk, and enjoy each other's company. I took her to the old dam site, which everybody called the Snake Hole due to the rattlesnakes near there. We walked down only to find eight people butt naked!

I said, "we'll go to Texas Point at Christina Lake, instead." We arrived at Texas Point, only to find another group of people completely nude.

I was starting to wonder if we were ever going to find a private place for the two of us. I said, "okay, we'll go to the Joe Girl's Beach on the Kettle River." Turned out that the third place was the charm; no one was there. We swam and laughed. I felt bad about taking her to the swimming places where people were skinny dipping, not exactly the intimate setting I was going for. I apologized to her for the other two places I took her to. She laughed at the experience.

Slowly, but without a doubt, I was falling in love with her. We kept on dating. I told her that I was in love with her every waking moment, that I wanted to be with her. We felt so connected that I knew we were meant to be together. Sometimes having the bravery to speak your mind, no matter how scary it might be, pays off. She replied that the same thing was happening to her and she felt exactly the same way.

I asked her if I could buy her a ring, a going steady ring, and she said sure. I wanted her to know how much I loved her and wanted her in my life. We drove up to Charley's Jewelry Store, and I told her about a ring I had seen when I was five years old. I first saw it when my mom and I went there to pick up my dad's watch that had been repaired. The ring was a purple sapphire, the most beautiful I had ever seen. When we arrived at the store, I immediately saw it at the bottom of the display case, just as it had been for sixteen years. I pointed it out to her and we both laughed that the ring was still there. I bought it for her and she put it on her finger; it was too big, but later we had it sized to fit. Somehow I knew that ring had been there for sixteen years, waiting for the right time for me to buy it for this special lady, the love of my life.

We had been dating for a while before she told she had a two-year old daughter and asked me if I would like to meet her. I immediately said yes. I was so ready to settle down with this beautiful lady that a daughter was a bonus. I not only had this woman in my life, but also the possibility of a family. What more could a man ask for? I was thrilled at the prospect. We went to where she was living and her two-year old came into the room. Meredith said, "Ron, this is Terri."

Terri walked up to me, stuck out her tongue and said, "I don't like you."

I replied, "it's so nice to meet you, I'm Ron." That was the relationship Terri and I had for a while, but nothing discouraged me from working toward having a life with Meredith.

We decided to move into our own place. At one point in our relationship we wanted to get married, so when we moved into the upstairs of an old house on Central Avenue, one of the first things we did was say our vows to each other. To me this was my commitment to be with this woman for the rest of my life. I was grateful every day that God had answered my request and brought this wonderful, beautiful woman into my life.

Shortly after we said our vows in that old house, I officially asked her to marry me and she said yes. We started making plans and arrangements to get married in June of that year; we were both happy and excited. My life with Meredith was everything I had ever wanted. I did whatever I could to make her happy every day.

Over those first months of our relationship we talked about everything. I told her all about my life, my past, my dreams, and my out-of-body experiences. It was not the least bit surprising that she knew and understood what

I was talking about. She introduced me to the writings of Edgar Cayce, the sleeping prophet, who for years had been helping people with his visions, premonitions, and predictions while in a dream state. Meredith explained to me that my dreams and visions were a form of astral traveling. She showed me Lobsang Rampa's books and writings. He wrote about the phenomenon of astral projection. Meredith read all of them to me and, for the first time in my life, I could talk openly with someone about these things. The new information explained to me what I had been doing and seeing for many years. There were other people out there that were familiar with this experience. I was not alone!

We were living together from October to June and our wedding date had been set for June 7th. We were excited about our upcoming ceremony, but I knew there is something on her mind. In May, Meredith said, "I have two more children, two boys." Her boys were living in Calgary with a foster family.

"That's fantastic, but where are they?" I asked.

Meredith told me about the life of hell that she and her children had lived through with her ex-husband, and what had happened to create the situation where the boys were placed in foster care. When she was finally able to escape from her ex, she was a single mom with three children, trying to work and look after her kids. Meredith's dad saw that she was struggling to hold together a home for the children and also contending with the constant threat of her ex finding them. Not sure what he would do if he found them, Meredith's dad told her to put the children in foster care to keep them safe, so that is what she did. It was a very painful decision that she had struggled with, which is why it had taken her so long to tell me. She didn't want me to think badly of her, which just made me love her more. She told me that the people that were fostering her boys wanted to adopt them. We went together to the Social Services office, where all she had to do was sign the papers to give up custody. We sat there and the social worker showed her where she had to sign.

I looked at her and said, "I believe children should be with their mom or dad. Somehow, some way, we will make this work. Let's bring those boys home!"

It was definitely a process getting the boys back. Finally, after a lot of hard work, they came home. By this time, we were married and were fully prepared to make a happy home for the boys and Terri. It took Terri some time to warm up to me. She was not a trusting little soul and continued to stick her tongue out at me and tell me that she didn't like me, but that became less and less as time went on. One day I looked at her and said, "I only have to put up with you for another sixteen years and then some lucky young man will marry you... and you can stick your tongue out at him."

When Meredith told her family about everything that had occurred with her ex, my brother-in-law said that the next time he saw him, he was going to smash his face in. Meredith's dad told me if he saw him again, he was going to put a bullet in his head. Meredith told me her dad had helped them out early in their relationship by co-signing for their house, their car, and their boat. At one point, her ex decided it was time to leave town since he had pulled some shady deal and had to leave quickly. He forced Meredith to leave in the middle of the night, abandoning everything they owned including their pets, and also left her dad carrying the debts they had incurred that totalled near forty thousand dollars. That was a lot of money in those days and her parents were still raising kids at home, so it caused a great deal of hardship for the family for a number of years. Everybody in Meredith's family seemed to hate her ex-husband, for one reason or another.

I'm glad he was a total asshole, otherwise I might never have found Meredith. Life was great and we had a beautiful family! Because of my beautiful wife, I now understood who I was. As my dreams continued, I now understood why it was happening, but still wondered, *why me?*

CHAPTER TWENTY

THE LEPRECHAUN

We had our happy little family and Meredith would read a lot of stories to the kids. One night she was reading to them so I went outside with a cup of coffee and sat on the step of the porch to relax. There are three pine trees in the corner of the yard, and when I looked toward them, I saw the grass move. I kept looking and finally saw this four-inch little being. He was dressed in black and wearing a black hat with a brass buckle, black pants, black shoes also with brass buckles on them, and he had a beard. I watched him walk from one tree to another, disappearing behind each one. I went inside and told Meredith what I had just seen. She believed me and we went out and looked for a hole around the trees, but never found anything. I often wonder where he came from and where he went. Another of those odd, unexplainable events in my life!

CHAPTER TWENTY-ONE

THE SPEAR-LIKE SHARD

In 1975, I was falling trees for a logging contractor by the name of Stewart Walker. It had always been my habit to move to a safe spot as the tree fell, a habit that had saved me more times than I can count in my career as a logger.

To my left was a balsam tree, about two feet away. As the tree fell, it bent at the twenty-foot mark, where there was also Jack pine, bent so that the top of the tree was touching the ground.

All of a sudden, I heard a snap, then a thud! I looked to my left and a piece of the Jack pine, three feet long, flew back at me and stuck into a tree to my left. Luckily, I wasn't standing in front of it or I would have been speared right in the neck. That would've been a total mess, finding me dead in the bush. Logging is not without its risks, you have to always pay attention to every movement and sound and it just might save your life, as it certainly has for me.

But accidents happen all the time and, that same day, I started my undercut when a piece of rock hit my left eye. I knew I needed medical attention, so I went to see my boss and he immediately drove me to the hospital. My wife met me there and Dr. Nielson, the local doctor on call that day, said to Meredith, "take Ron to Kelowna Hospital." He told me I should lie flat on my back as we went to the neighbouring town.

We drove to Kelowna right away, me lying flat on my back during the trip. When we arrived, they made me lie on my back again. My eye looked pretty bad; there was a purple area, which was full of blood. The doctors and nurses in Kelowna were very concerned and said they didn't know if they could save the eye. I had to stay in the hospital for awhile in order for them to treat my injury. However, once again, I was very lucky as my eye healed after two weeks.

Meredith came to visit with me while I was in the hospital, which I didn't like very much. I was finally able to go home, where my sweet wife took care of me. I missed her every moment I was in the hospital and was so glad to be home. The time spent away was more torture than the pain of my injury.

CHAPTER TWENTY-TWO

ROSES AND BUTTERFLIES

This one night, I was astral travelling and I noticed this planet. I decided to go in that direction to take a look. It was indescribably beautiful! I had never seen anything like it on this Earth. As far as the eye could see, there appeared to be gentle, rolling hills entirely covered in red, long-stem roses about three feet tall. The leaves were similar to the roses on Earth. Some were in bloom and some about to bloom, but I noticed that none of them were dead or browned from age. The colors were so bright and vivid, exuding the life within each flower, that each bloom was intoxicating in their beauty. They had a magnetic effect, making you want to look closer at each flower.

Upon each of the roses, flying between and above them thirty feet in the air, were thousands of butterflies of all colors, shapes, and forms.

I was so taken by the scene in front of me, and I did not see any other types of animals there. I did not look for anything between the roses or past the hills. I remember thinking that there was so much more to see, but I was so taken by the roses and the butterflies, I just wanted to drink in the beauty of the scene in front of my eyes.

I suddenly awoke from my dream state, feeling this sense of amusement at what I had just witnessed and experienced. What a privilege it had been to go there and see such wonder, such beauty.

One day, I hope to consciously return to that planet, and explore its vast horizons. I hope to be more aware of where the planet is located in conjunction to Earth. I remember thinking, *what a beautiful planet, how far am I from home?* I hope to know the directions of my travel when I get there, and re-visit the most beautiful place I've ever seen.

CHAPTER TWENTY-THREE

LIGHTNING

In 1976 I was still working as a faller for Stewart Walker. One day there was a hell of a storm, raining, snowing, hailing, the thunder booming, and there was lightning everywhere. I was standing back in the timber, trying to stay out of it as best as I could.

The lightening was striking all around us coming down into the trees, and I could see there were veins of electricity going right through the branches. The veins were coming toward me so I backed up, thinking I was going to get struck by lightning and needed to get out of this. A slow moving vein of lightening about one inch thick went under my chin and past my throat. The lightning was everywhere, and I thought to myself, *how do I get out of here and make my escape?* There was nowhere to go, nowhere to run; I was pretty much stuck there, just having to wait out the storm and hope I could survive.

Finally, after what seemed like forever, the storm just stopped. I put my saw down and covered it with my rain jacket. I checked myself and discovered I was no worse for the experience. There weren't any injuries and I had amazingly made it through that.

I decided I needed to get back to the crew, so I headed to the crummy. When I got in, a crew-member asked, "where have you been? We've been waiting for you for over half an hour."

They thought the lightning had killed me. It was close, but I was still standing. I've never seen lightening move in slow motion through the trees like that before.

Another stormy day, I was raking in the yard on the west side of the house. Meredith was looking out the window watching me as I raked twenty feet from the house, looking west. Behind me, a lightning bolt struck right to the ground. Meredith yelled out, "are you okay??" I replied that I was and Meredith said, "I thought it hit you."

That was how close it had come to me, and she was very happy that I was still alive. Luckily, I was wearing leather work boots that day and I never felt the shock of the close call. Nature is a mysterious, wondrous thing. There are many unexplainable occurrences that happen in nature, and it lets people know how powerful nature can be. A power that I definitely have a great deal of healthy respect for.

CHAPTER TWENTY-FOUR

NICK ON THE CAT

A year later I was out falling trees, working strips on a logging block. Everyone else was skidding trees 100 yards away from me. The brush was twelve feet high, and I was making sure not to fall anything but the trees. All of a sudden I noticed the brush behind me being slapped to the ground, and a Cat blade appear just eight feet behind me. Nick, the operator, couldn't see me and I knew I needed to get his attention before he ran over me.

I threw my hardhat at the Cat and it stopped. I climbed up on the treads and told Nick, "you almost killed me!"

Nick says, "I didn't see you."

"Nick, go over there 100 yards away and stay there!"

He said okay, turned the Cat around, and left. I went back to falling the trees until twenty minutes later, once again the brush behind me almost hit me and I saw the Cat blade coming right for me. I was in the middle of pounding a wedge in a tree. I turned around, threw my axe and hit the side of the Cat. The Cat stopped and I climbed up. "You son of a bitch," I screamed. "What are you doing here? You almost ran over me! Nick, I just told you to go somewhere else, didn't I?"

"Ron, I'm sorry, I don't know why I came back here," Nick replied.

"Nick, I've thrown my hard hat at you. I've thrown my axe. If you come back again, I'm going to throw my power saw at you!" Nick did not come back, but he had almost killed me twice within an hour!

Logging is a dangerous business, people lose their lives due to nature, due to the conditions you are working under, and then there is simple human error. People don't pay attention, and if you work in the bush you have to constantly be watching everything and everyone.If you're not aware of your surroundings you won't survive. Too many good people have lost their lives in the bush! I am grateful not to be one of those people, but I have seen a lot of situations and experienced a number of injuries in the years while working up on those mountains. I stayed safe and alive because I always paid attention to everything around and above me at all times.

CHAPTER TWENTY-FIVE

CLOSE CALLS

One morning I was on my way to work, around 2:30 a.m. My regular route to work, I would drive on 2nd Street to the intersection where the Grand Forks Hotel was on my right, and another building on my left.

Each morning, I would drive to this intersection, I would wait for the light to change, and turn left as soon as it changed. But that morning the light changed to green and, for no good reason, I hesitated for a second or two. A car went flying by, right through the red light! I didn't see him coming!

I got that feeling in my gut that told me I had just missed a disaster. That car would have creamed me if I had pulled out earlier. I crept forward, slowly looking both ways, and then turned left onto Central Avenue. When I got home after work, I heard that the car I had seen that morning had flown off the bridge and the car had been totaled, killing the driver. It was a good lesson for me though, and to this day when the red light changes to green, I slowly pull out.

One day, working for Stewart West Log Company, I found myself ahead on the falling schedule. The Cat driver didn't show up, so my boss Stewart asked me if I would drive the Cat and I said yes. The machine was parked, but running. I got on and Stewart pointed to the brake. "That's the brake and that's the emergency," he said. "Now go down that trail." Which I did.

It was a steep and narrow trail, and I was going like hell down it when I stepped on the brake. The pedal hit the floor. There were no brakes! I pulled the emergency brake and it came right out of where it was attached. The Cat was accelerating and I had no control, so I stood up and bailed out. The Cat went another fifty feet, then over the bank. I looked over the bank and watched it disappear into the timber. After a couple of seconds, I heard a loud bang. I walked back to the landing and Stewart asked, "where's the Cat?"

"It's down there somewhere over the bank," I said to him. "Did you know it had no brakes and no emergency brake? That's probably why the driver never came to work."

Another time working for Stewart, a tree fell across a ten-foot-deep draw. I walked out on it and was going to give it a little cut in the middle to make it easier to skid out. I cut two inches on one side and two inches on the other. The tree suddenly snapped and I went down with it. I was standing in limbs up to my waist as my saw went flying upwards with the throttle locked. I couldn't run anywhere. The saw started coming down at me and I thought it was going to get me in the neck. When it was a foot away, I took my left hand and pushed my right hand toward it. It hit my right hand and cut in as I pushed away. There was blood everywhere. I shut the saw off, took my T-shirt, wrapped it tightly around the cut, and walked to the landing.

"I need a ride down, I've been cut," I said to Stewart as I arrived. He went into a total panic. "I've got the bleeding under control."

We got into his truck and he blasted us out of there, sliding around the corners. "Stewart, slow down or you're going to kill us both!" I yelled. He slowed down somewhat, but he was still frantic. Eventually we somehow made it to the hospital. The nurse scrubbed the two slices clean. Dr. Valin froze the two-inch cuts and started suturing the wound. I complimented him, saying, "those are the best stitches I've ever had." They dressed the wound well and the next morning Meredith put clean dressing on the thirty stitches.

I have never been the kind of person who can stay off work. If I can walk and I can breathe, I will be at work, regardless of what doctors have told me. With that in mind, I returned to work the next morning, even though Dr. Valin said I would be off for two or three weeks. Stewart was surprised to see me. He couldn't believe I would come back to work after such an injury.

At that time, I was falling 75 to 85 loads every ten days. I was making good money compared to Worker's Compensation pay. In three weeks, Meredith took out my stitches, as she had done many times before.That power saw coming at me full throttle could have killed me! I consider myself lucky I only ended up with some cuts on my hands and a few stitches.

I was always trying to fall more trees every day, constantly striving to outdo myself. I continued to fall 80 and sometimes 85 loads in ten days, still working for Stewart West Logging at the back end of the Burrell Creek Area.

Where we were working, the thought crossed my mind and I wondered if it was possible to fall 100 loads in ten days. The ground was good and the timber was 100 feet tall. I was running from tree to tree, absolutely determined to beat my record.

In nine days I had 90 loads hauled out, and I kept up my pace. The tenth day, nine loads had been hauled out and there was one more truck that should've come, which would make it 100 loads. The truck never came. The next day, I found out the driver decided to buy a bottle of whiskey and go home early.

Years later, I was still trying to beat my record. At this one site, the ground and the timber were perfect and I managed to get 101 loads out in ten days. Being stubborn, my goal was 100 loads even, and I promised myself that I would hit that number precisely.

One of my co-workers, Winnipeg George, said to me one day, "I can outfall you, let's have a competition."

"When you fall 99 to 101 loads in ten days, give me a call." I'm still waiting for his call to come in.

When I got off work, Meredith greeted me with a wonderful kiss and a hug and told me she saw a double rainbow in the sky above our house. She ran inside, got the camera, and took a picture, which I still have.

CHAPTER TWENTY-SIX

IN THE TREES

I have always been a great believer that everything happens for a reason. One day, Stewart decided to phone his boss and give him all kinds of verbal crap. The next morning, a supervisor from the sawmill told us that because of Stewart's words to his boss, they were moving us to the top of the mountain. There was ten feet of snow, the trees were covered in ice, and were almost frozen to the ground. I would be lucky to fall 60 loads in ten days. It was 25 degrees Fahrenheit or colder and I was working as hard as I could to keep warm.

To my right was the edge of the block. I glanced over and noticed a dead tree five feet above the snow. On top of the tree was a small, three-foot being. He was wearing a red shirt, light-blue pants, curled toed boots, and a red toque. His cheeks were red, and as he breathed, there was steam coming from his mouth. I pinched my face and I could feel it, confirming that I was awake. I looked at him and waved. *Where did he come from? Somewhere on this mountain, must be his home.* I went back to work. I was thinking I had just seen something very unusual. Every now and again I'd look over there, and after twenty minutes, I looked again, and he was gone.

If my boss hadn't gone on his tirade, I would not have been there to have seen it. I told Meredith what I saw, and as always she believed me. I often wonder what I will see next that is unexplained or unusual.

It wasn't long before I was up in the bush one day, falling trees just below a new road that had been blasted. All of the treetops had also been blasted off. Chunks of treetops were in the trees I was falling, and I had to be careful that none would fall on me.

I always like to be on the left side of the tree when I'm falling. I came up to a two-foot spruce and went to the left side to fall it down the hill. I stood there for a moment and thought, *there's something wrong here!* I didn't know what the danger was and I looked at the tree again. There weren't any broken tops that could tumble and kill me, but that feeling continued.

My intuition was telling me not to stand on the left side, so I went to the right side of the tree instead. I started cutting in the undercut and a 250 lb. rock fell on the left side of the tree, right where I was standing.

CHAPTER TWENTY-SEVEN

UNIDENTIFIED OBJECTS

We were all going on a family outing, including Meredith, her sons Rick and Ron, and Terri. We decided to go for a drive to see her sister, Peggy, and her husband Norman. They were living in a trailer at Almond Garden's Trailer Park, just outside of Grand Forks.

Meredith and her sister were chatting, so Norman and I went outside to drink beer and enjoy the nice evening. The sky was perfectly clear. Norman says, "look at that bright light in the sky, it has small red dots leaving it." The light formed an exact triangle and was very bright. We started joking around and saying, "come on down and have a beer with us!" We didn't think much about the craft in the sky; it could have been a satellite, a star, or just a plane.

When it was time to go home, we all got into the car. Meredith was driving and we were heading east on Carson Road when we noticed there was a bright light above us, maybe one mile away. It seemed to be following us. At the end of Carson Road, we turned down onto North Ruckle, and the light appeared to continue to follow us. We arrived at the house we were renting from Alec Davidoff, near the Grand Forks Sawmill. Meredith parked the car and the three kids went into the house with us following behind. We got into the house and noticed the family cat with its back is arched up in the air and its hair on end like it had licked a socket. It was making a very strange sound and we thought the cat had gone crazy. It was going in circles, continuing to make all kinds of weird sounds with its back arched upward.

We got the kids settled in, and then went outside to sit on the step to have a cigarette. We looked over at the sawmill. On the east side, near the mill and approximately sixty feet from the ground was what appeared to be the top of a plane. It was eighty feet long and forty feet wide. It looked very similar to a stealth fighter jet; charcoal black and not shiny. The front had three windows, there were dull lights of red, blue, and green. There appeared to be a figure moving back and forth in the front windows. We watched for about twenty minutes. The craft would slowly lean to the left and then level off again.

Meredith says, "do you think I should phone the police?"

"Sure, but they might think you are crazy." I had to work the next day, so I went to bed.

Meredith told me she watched, and after a while it slowly rose up into the sky and disappeared. It made no sense to either of us, why this thing would be flying above the mill. Someone in the sawmill should have seen it. Apparently, there were a few people talking about seeing *something* in the sky afterward, but

I think we had the best view. Being an artist, Meredith decided to draw a sketch of it; she wanted to capture what we had seen on paper. The day after, when I came home from work, the cat was back to its normal self as well.

Another time, a man in his 50's and myself were in a tree-planting camp. It was a nice clear day. I looked up and the sky turned to a light purple. Something started forming in the sky, what appeared like yellow drops of ink in the shape of a "Y."

I watched as it was forming and said to the man, "Isn't that something?"

"Yep, the sky is sure blue today," he replied.

A few minutes went by and the "Y" disappeared. I often wondered what that meant and why the other fellow didn't see it. The "Y" was at least 100 feet in length and 50 feet wide at the top, and he never mentioned it.

CHAPTER TWENTY-EIGHT

GROWING AN ALREADY HAPPY FAMILY

Meredith and I had been married five years when we have decided to have children of our own. We lived in a 1974 Leader mobile home with two mobile additions. There was seven acres of land with Ponderosa pine on it. Meredith was close to her due date, and since she had already had three children, I was sure she would tell me when it was time to go to the hospital.

She turned to me and said, "Dear one, it's time to go to the hospital."

I got the car running so it would be nice and warm. We walked down the steps and her water broke. "We won't make it to the hospital," she informed me. I took her back into the bedroom, she laid down, and I called the hospital.

"My wife is having a baby right now. Can you give me a course on how to deliver the baby?"

"Feel to see if the cord is around the baby's neck. If it is, move it," the nurse said. "When the baby is born and if the umbilical cord is still attached to the mother, do not panic as the baby is getting oxygen from it." The nurse told me that she had sent an ambulance. I told the nurse I was going to attempt it, and left the phone on the counter.

I went back to the bedroom and, sure enough, the cord was around the baby's neck. I flipped it over, and there came the baby, his cord still attached. My son, Jesse, looked at me and smiled! I put him on Meredith's chest and she held him close. The ambulance driver and attendant came in with a stretcher and told me they had never dealt with this before, but they did very well.

I went back to the phone and told the nurse that the baby was fine, and Meredith and Jesse were on their way to the hospital. The nurse and I both laughed and I thanked her for the quick course on how to deliver the baby. I then called someone in the family to watch the three older kids. As soon as I could, I went to see Meredith and my new son. We just laughed with joy. Meredith was in the hospital for three days. Jesse weighed 8 ½ lbs. and Meredith was a petite woman, normally weighing 100 lbs. But somehow, she managed to deliver this little person. In the next three days, I made a cradle for Jesse, happy to have another addition to our family.

CHAPTER TWENTY-NINE

DECEMBER 31ST, 1980: JAMES IS BORN

Meredith was due to have our second baby anytime that day. This time I wasn't taking any chance of not making it to the hospital; delivering one baby in a lifetime was enough for me! She had a few pains and I got the car running and warmed up. It was 1:00 a.m. when she started having more contractions. I helped her into the car and we were off to the hospital.

When we arrived at the hospital, Dr. Nielson said, not yet. We headed back home and kept the car running in the yard. At 3:40 a.m., I helped her back into the car, her pains really close together. Dr. Nielson was still there, and by 4:15, we had delivered the baby.

It was a beautiful baby boy; James, our second son! It was a wonderful day, as I got to be there when he was born. James was six weeks premature and we prayed we wouldn't lose him. He was only four and a half pounds, but went down to four pounds. Thank God he eventually made it. We were so happy and grateful. James was in the hospital for over a month before we were able to finally bring him home to our family!

CHAPTER THIRTY

VISIONS

One night, I found myself in space. To my left I could see the earth below me; North and South America were visible to me. I looked forward and saw mist forming right in front of me. A small, winged angel appeared and floated toward the mist, kicking one of its legs to move closer to the cloud. With every kick, I could hear a sound, "re-ar-ah-re-ar ah."

Two more angels materialized, then two more. A different type of being appeared wearing a long gown and holding a scroll in its left hand. Three of the angels hovered on its right and two on its left. One of the angels came right to my face to get my attention, then went back to the being's left-hand side and began looking at the scroll.

The mist formed a type of funnel: from the bottom of it, two long streamers of mist went toward the earth and formed a left and right hand, so that the mist was now holding the planet. The being continued looking down at the scroll as it floated over the funnel, slowly unraveling the parchment. I could tell that the being was reading the scroll, its eyes tracking from left to right. I noticed that, as all five angels were looking down, they were all identical in their physicality and facial expressions.

I instinctively knew that a message was being sent to earth, but couldn't hear any words spoken by the being. The scroll was finally fully open when the being stopped. A few moments passed before I decided to move closer to the being's forty-foot high head. At a closer proximity, I could see that its skin was a medium gray, while the angels had human-looking skin.

I looked down at the being's left hand into a single pore of its skin. The more I concentrated, the more my gaze plumbed the endless depths, the skin transforming into different shapes and sizes; an eternal Fibonacci spiral of geometric designs cast in a refracted blue light. I inherently knew that if I looked into the other pores, I would find more of the same.

I saw the colors very clearly: blue, white, green, mauve, all reflecting within the endless depth. I moved back to where I had been floating and the being and the arms of mist holding the earth slowly dissipated. The angels turned, kicking one leg to propel themselves away. I awoke in my bed, conscious and aware, the vision still so clearly in my mind.

The next morning, Meredith woke me up and we had coffee while I told her about my dream. Since we were so connected to each other, I knew she would understand what I was about to tell her. I described the vision and she asked a few questions about the size of the being and the angels. After I explained, she picked up a pencil and started to sketch. After a few minutes, I looked at what she'd done; it was almost perfect. I told her that the lips of the being were too close, so she adjusted it just a little and it was exactly what I had seen the night before. I wondered what the message was for our planet.

(In the vision the scroll could have represented "The Book of Life" or the "Akashic Record")

Another night, I was in bed asleep and I began to dream...

I was looking east from the porch when I saw a large charcoal grey asteroid. It was flying over the valley, and I estimated that it was four miles in width and three miles in length. I couldn't see the end of it, only the front as it neared the mountains to the south. I couldn't see the thickness, but it looked to be close to a mile. As it headed southward, I wondered, *is this part of the Hopi Prophecy?* I looked at a globe and tried to figure out the trajectory. After a few quick calculations, I determined that it was heading for the island where the metal pole stands as it's stopping point. As the asteroid passed over, I noticed there was no burning tail, making me think it must be made of ice.

In a third vision that I had around that time, I found myself in my backyard wearing snowshoes. There was approximately 40 feet of snow, and I could also see a star-shaped circular walkway made of snow leading down to our root cellar. When I awoke, I told Meredith about this and planted a large garden. From it, we dried squash and other vegetables and herbs, and then went out and bought two tons of wheat, thinking this apocalypse could happen to our world at any time. After a while, life continued on as it always had and we eventually sold the wheat and relaxed. There was no way to predict when this could happen, and trying to wait for the end of the world is not worth the stress.

I often wonder, *what will I see next? What does it all mean? What will be the next unexplainable vision/dream I will experience?*

CHAPTER THIRTY-ONE

SAND CREEK

Meredith and I eventually formed our own company. I was a Falling Contractor and Meredith did all the bookwork, bill paying, and running of the business.

I was out on a job, wearing knee-pads that cover the knees and go almost up to your thighs, which will save your legs from a power-saw cut. Somehow that day, the saw bucked back and cut my right leg just above the knee pad guard, six inches across. I took my T-shirt and wrapped the wound. I asked one of my employees, Gordie Rod, to drive me down the mountain. He was in a total panic, so I told him, "The bleeding is under control, everything's fine." Gordie wasn't convinced, he was driving like a maniac and I had to tell him to slow down or he is going to kill both of us.

Gordie wanted to drive me directly to the hospital. I said I wanted to be driven home, and he complied. Meredith was worried about the wound. I got into the shower and cleaned it up and Meredith wrapped the cut and drove me to the hospital. We arrived at the hospital, they got me onto a stretcher, and a nurse scrubbed the wound to remove the bits of sawdust and debris. The doctor came in and, after freezing the area, used over twenty-five staples to suture the gash. The doctor released me and told me to stay home for at least three weeks.

The next day, Meredith helped me bandage the wound with tensor bandages, then I drove up to Sand Creek and went back to work. My leg was as stiff as a board. My boss was surprised to see me there. After a week, my leg limbered up and I could bend it and move around a lot more.

After three weeks passed, the wound looked really good and Meredith helped me take out the staples. We used sterilized side cutters to cut the staples in half and then took them out. Meredith took all the stitches out as she had done many times before. Unfortunately, my skin had grown over two of the staples. I had to miss half of a day of work to get them taken out at the hospital. The Doctor asked me how many days of work I had missed. I told him it was one and a half days, plus the half day I was missed to get the last two staples removed. He gave me a strange look, and I thanked him for what he did and walked out.

When it comes to wounds, I have always found that getting movement and the blood circulating promotes healing faster. Meredith always took out my stitches from my many injuries. In addition to being my lovely, beautiful wife, she was also my doctor and nurse.

CHAPTER THIRTY-TWO

THE LAST SUPPER

Despite how surreal many of my experiences have been, some may have a hard time believing this next chapter. We had a hard time believing it ourselves and we were there, so believe me when I say that every word is true!

Meredith and I were out sitting on the steps having a coffee and a cigarette at about 10:00 a.m. one morning. There was a storm forming over the east side of the valley, slightly to the north. Some of the clouds were black as coal, some white as snow, and some had different hues of grey. We assumed there was one hell of a storm coming.

The clouds stopped and began to swirl, similar to a tornado, but there were multiple groups of clouds adding to this swirling motion; clouds don't normally do that. The different coloured clouds were swirling towards each other, converging on a central position, with little swirls extended in every direction.

We had never seen anything like this before in our lives. The swirls concentrated to an area about three hundred feet wide at a height of fifty feet. We put our coffee cups down and walked a little bit to stand with our fence in front of us, and fifty-foot pines behind. The swirls intensified and continued to spiral toward each other. I turned to Meredith, "I have never seen anything like this before." She replied that neither had she.

I asked if the camera was handy. She said, "yes, but the batteries are dead."

The swirls stopped and two large tables started to appear in the clouds, then baskets of food and cups. People appeared: six on the left and five on the right.

There was one being standing almost in the centre point. On the left-hand side was a man with a beard, and the man second from far right was also bearded.

I looked at the man to the left of the central being, and noticed that he was looking down and slightly to the left. The man in the centre appeared to be tall, and gave off this sense of kindness. He was smiling, almost like he was joking with the person sitting to his left. The entire scene was grey.

This feeling came over me that I shouldn't look at the men any more. When I looked down to their feet, I could see the fine woven toe holds of their sandals. The detail of the entire scene was outstanding, we watched this for two to three minutes, before the scene slowly dissipated and the clouds disappeared.

Meredith and I looked at each other in awe. I said to her, "you are a better person than me, I think that was for you. This is something the Pope or some religious leader should have seen, why us?" Meredith called her sister, Sandy, and told her what she saw. The detail with which she described it made Sandy believe her.

To see that image form out of clouds in such detail was spectacular. Meredith and I have never heard of anybody else seeing or experiencing this. Odds are that there have to be others who have, we've just never encountered them. To this day, when I see clouds of a storm forming in the sky, I look to see if they will form anything else. When I am driving and I see a storm of clouds, I will pull over and watch them, and then when nothing happens, I move on. Meredith, who was an artist and could draw this in exact detail, never did! We talked about this many times, and to this day, every now and then, I look up into the sky at that exact spot and say to myself, *wow, wasn't that something!*

CHAPTER THIRTY-THREE

101 UNIQUES & ANTIQUES AND A CRY FOR HELP

Meredith opened up an antique store in our home: *101 Uniques & Antiques.* I helped by refinishing and restoring furniture as well hauling truckloads of furniture to auction houses in Vancouver, Chilliwack, and Langley.

My vivid dreams still continued to occur, but I had become able to shut out most of them. However, one night I saw a dark haired woman in her late twenties calling out for help. I didn't know who or where she was, but I could see a house with a bench at the end of the street on the right-hand side. I saw a man talking on the telephone, looking south through a large window. I felt like he was talking about killing someone.

The next evening at around 11:00 p.m., I drove to Vancouver to Maynard's Auction House with a load of furniture. On my return, I stopped in Hope for gas and went inside to order something to eat. I looked up when I heard a woman call for help. There was a man of about 5'8" walking out of the kitchen. I was looking right at him and could see that he was balding on the front of his head, with scraggly hair on the back. I sensed this was the man who was hurting the woman.

The next day in Grand Forks, I went into the R.C.M.P. office and told them about my dream and the woman calling for help. I gave them a detailed description of the man coming out of the restaurant kitchen and told them I thought he was the one hurting the woman.

The R.C.M.P. officer recorded my statement on tape, even though I got the sense that the Mountie thought I was a nut case and was humoring me. Two years later, I looked up at the television and saw the man I'd seen coming out of the restaurant kitchen in Hope. The news station identified him as Robert Pickton, the serial killer.

CHAPTER THIRTY-FOUR

MEREDITH: MY WIFE, MY LIFE

Being married to Meredith was always wondrous. She was not only gorgeous, but talented in so many ways. At twelve years old, she was a pianist and played Bach, Beethoven, and more. She was an artist: her mediums were oils, pastels, pencil, charcoal, and pencil crayon. She also did bead work, leather work, baskets, poetry...the list goes on. I have most of her art; a number of pieces are displayed in our early 1900's cabin.

Meredith grew up in Moose Jaw, Saskatchewan. She loved her first love, but he did not love her. That ended but she had his child, Richard. She then met another man, ten years older than her. They had a son named Ron and a daughter named Terri.

They were constantly moving, escaping unpaid bills or enemies her ex had made along the way. They moved from Moose Jaw to Northern Manitoba, then to St. Paul, Minnesota, then to Vancouver Island. He was constantly cheating on her, always in the bars and conning whoever he could to get work or money. He did everything he could to destroy the relationship. Finally one day, he left for a job out of town, giving Meredith her chance. She packed up the three children and left. Her family kept her safe from him. He was more than just disliked; he wasn't trusted by any of the family. Meredith's father said she couldn't take care of all three children and work, so Richard and Ron went into foster care.

Meredith then moved to Grand Forks, where she lived with Peggy and Norman, as well as her sister, Sandy and her husband Dwain. Her other sister, Susan, was married and living in Calgary at that time.

Meredith's dad was the postmaster at the Grand Forks Post Office. Meredith's mom and dad and three brothers lived above the post office. Meredith's dad was later transferred to Golden to take over the postmaster's position there.

This is where I met her, fell in love, and got married to her. I loved her with all of my heart, our life was always wondrous, beautiful, and the best years of my life.

CHAPTER THIRTY-FIVE

THE OLD GREEN HOUSE

One Saturday, I was out looking for yard sales, trying to find antiques for Meredith's antique store. Two hundred yards past the OK Tire, there was a sign stating yard sale on the left side of the highway. I pulled in a saw an old, green, two-storey house. As I started buying old pieces of country furniture, I noticed a for sale sign for the property. I asked Helen the owner, "is it just the two storey house?"

"No," she replied. "There is a smaller house as well. And lots of space." I asked her the price and she told me. I drove out of the yard and straight to the realtor. I walked in and said I was interested in the property and wanted to put down a deposit of $100.00. The realtor laughed, and said, "that's not enough."

I replied, "It is. It's a legal deposit." Having no argument against that, he gave me a receipt.

When I got home, Meredith wasn't there. I left and found her car at the thrift store. Just as I was entering, she walked out and asked if I found anything at the yard sales. I replied, "Yes, I bought some furniture and I bought the property." She laughed, and I told her I put $100.00 deposit down. I said, "If you like the property, we'll buy it. But if you don't, then I've lost $100.00." We went back to the house and Helen gave us a tour of the place. Meredith liked the property and said it would be a great place for her antique store, being right on the highway. Our credit was good and the credit union gave us the money, making us the new owners of the house on the highway!

After cleaning and painting the little house, we moved in and started work on the big green one. I was upstairs in the big house, painting away, and I decided to look up in the attic. I got a ladder and climbed up into the attic. When I reached the far end, I could hear someone singing. I thought Meredith had come upstairs and put on some music. I came back down, only to find no one was there. I went downstairs and found Meredith in the little house. I asked her if she had come upstairs into the big house and put on some music, and she said no. When I told her about the music, we laughed and said maybe it was singing Bill, one of the occupants that had passed away.

Going down to the basement of the big house, the stairway descends halfway, then changes in a ninety degree direction to the basement floor. I was at the turning point of the stairs and stopped to inspect the old planks of the floor. I felt a hand on top of my left shoulder, and turned only to see no one there. I told Meredith, and again we laughed, excited at the prospect of living somewhere haunted.

Meredith decided to paint a border around the floor in one of the rooms upstairs: lines around the outer edges of the room and diamonds to accent the floor. She did a fantastic end centerpiece, leaving the remaining floor intact. We started to decorate each room with a theme. The first room at the top of the stairs was a sitting room with settees and chairs, small tables and pictures, and small antique glassware to accent the room. The next room on the left was decorated with all handmade Doukhobor furniture, rugs, spinning wheel, clothing, wooden bowls, and ladies clothing; it was gorgeous.

Across from that room was James' room. At the end of the hall on the left-hand side was our son, Jesse's room. At the end, on the right, we put in a high post bed with spiral turnings, an old Chinese rug on the floor, a washstand with a bowl and pitcher, a few small tables, and antique pictures. Every room was beautiful since Meredith was so great at decorating. She and I had our bedroom downstairs, along with a cozy living room, a laundry room, and a small kitchen. Meredith did amazing folk art on all of the cupboards. There was also a large addition on the southeast corner of the house, and a carport.

Meredith and I were in the kitchen one day, when she laughed and said, "I hope the ghost likes what we've done, but if not, too bad." We heard a loud slap on the counter, like the sound made by a wooden spoon.

"Well," I said, "we are not alone here!"

James had his friend over one night. They went into James' room to find the ghostly figure of a tall, old man standing there. It scared the heck out of them at first, but they still went into the room after the initial shock, feeling that it was a friendly ghost, and no cause for concern.

Meredith's sister, Sandy, came down for a few days with her husband and Meredith showed them the end bedroom with the high-post bed. Later on that night, Sandy saw the tall ghost and told Meredith about it in the morning. Like James, Sandy wasn't bothered by the presence.

We decided to make the upstairs of the big house into a museum, thinking it would generate some money. We had a tenant in the little house and we moved the antiques into the upstairs of the big house, the boy's bedrooms, and stored antiques in the addition as well.

The house was freezing cold, so we put in an 1800 square foot gas fireplace. It was still cold, and we would get all of the electric baseboard heaters going all the time, but the place wouldn't warm up. We used the wood heater in the addition to help heat the house, but to no avail. I put an electric heater in the basement to keep the pipes from freezing and warm the floor, and it was still cold. When winter came, we burned through six cords of firewood. The wood heat, the gas fireplace, and baseboard heaters seemed to do nothing. Our entire family would be wearing heavy double wool socks, long underwear, and sweaters to keep warm. The back door from the addition kept opening by itself. The china cabinet doors wouldn't stay shut. I would just speak out loud and ask the ghost to close the doors, please, but they kept opening. Eventually, we got used to it, and weren't bothered by the ghost. We felt that the ghost was Helen's husband or one of her family members; someone who possibly died there.

One day, two ladies came in to buy some antiques. They went upstairs to look around, and when they came back down, they had a nice old 8-day clock that they wanted to purchase. One woman said to me with tears in her eyes, "Do you know you have a ghost upstairs?"

I said to her, "you've got to be kidding! A ghost?"

"He's a tall man." The woman paid for the clock and held it in her hands.

"Oh well," I said, trying to minimize our spectre. Just then, the back door and china cabinet opened at the same time. The two ladies never ever came back.

Meredith and I were not afraid. The ghost liked the Doukhobor room, and it just hung out there.

We decided to put both of our properties up for sale: the one with the big green house and small house on Highway #3, and also our house and property on Sagamore Road. We thought, *whichever one sells, we'll live in the other.* The big green house on the highway sold. At times, we would look back at our time there and just laugh, especially about the two ladies who bought the clock. The wooden spoon hitting the counter, the tapping on my shoulder, the singing upstairs, and the opening doors really were a wonderful experience for all of us. I think the ghost had a great sense of humor.

I often wonder how he is getting along with his new tenants, or if he left. Both my sister-in-law, Sandy, and my son, James, have never forgotten what they saw.

CHAPTER THIRTY-SIX

CADETS AND GENEALOGY

Meredith got a job in the post office and worked there for a while. Throughout our life together, she had been a traffic control person and worked at one of the local grocery stores, but by the time we had James, she was my partner and bookkeeper in our various logging and contract falling business.

The older kids were all doing well: Richard was in Air Cadets for a while, but changed over to Sea

Cadets, and Meredith got very involved, organizing for the Phoenix Sea Cadet corps. That took her to

Vancouver Island and she was promoted to Sub-Lieutenant and Officer in the Canadian Armed Forces Reserves. She was the Commanding Officer of the Sea Cadets, which included not only Richard, but Ron and Terri as well. Under her leadership, she had over twenty or more recruits.

Meredith would proudly march past the cenotaph on Remembrance Day. She would take her troop to Comox on Vancouver Island. They went on small ships called YAGs and went up the coast for two weeks or more at a time. The cadets took sailing courses and had shooting competitions. Being an officer, Meredith shot pistols and rifles.

Jesse and James were still quite young, and I would take care of them when she was gone with the cadets. I was so proud of her that I didn't mind parenting on my own while she was away.

An annual inspection came to Grand Forks. Commander Brent, the man in charge of the Canadian Forces came, giving Meredith an opportunity to proudly show off her cadets. Commander Brent gave Meredith a picture of himself to her. The next annual inspection, Admiral Yaro attended and he was very impressed. The admiral also presented Meredith with a picture of himself. Both photos hung in the cadet hall.

All of the cadets my dear Meredith worked with grew up and did very well as adults; no small credit goes to my wife.

At some point, Meredith decided to leave the Phoenix Squadron and turned it over to another officer. An officer from Comox came to our home and wanted her to remain in the Canadian Forces Reserves, but she decided she wanted to accomplish other goals in her life, so declined the invitation.

Our three older children went out on their own and started families, while Meredith and I are raised our two younger sons. She had her home based antique business going, which she enjoyed very much. She had an eye for antiques and the knowledge as well, and made a great living for several years due to her ability and expertise.

Meredith got very interested in her genealogy, as her dad said they were related to Pauline Johnson, and she spent many days and nights researching the family history, convinced she could find documentation to prove her native blood lines. Due to that research, she became involved with the local Metis

Association. She thoroughly enjoyed being part of the programs provided through the association, and she made lifelong friends through that involvement.

CHAPTER THIRTY-SEVEN

METIS UNITY RIDE AND RUN

One day, some of the Metis women dropped by to tell us that the Metis Unity Ride and Run was coming to Grand Forks, and they wanted to know if they could camp in our yard and forest. As always, of course, I supported all of my wife's ventures and agreed to let them camp out on our property. Meredith wasn't home at the time, and they needed her approval as well before they made the arrangements; they found her at the Thrift Store and it was, of course, a yes. We didn't know what to expect.

The Metis Unity Ride and Run participants arrived, riding in on horses. We had an open area that was about three-quarters of an acre. The participants rode around in a circle a few times, placed their "staff" into the ground, and dismounted. The staff was made of eagle feathers and claws that formed a handle.

The young runners and myself made a corral for the horses; we got hay and an old bathtub for water. Vehicles and small motorhomes rolled onto the property. The Chief and tribe introduced themselves to us, asked where they could park, and our front yard filled up with sixty Metis people.

They brought out their drums and started drumming. They drummed twenty-four hours a day for three days. The local Metis people started cooking up a storm: deer, moose, elk, all the delicacies of a true feast. The local chapter asked the Chief if the food was right and acceptable, and when he gave his blessing, everyone ate.

For the next day, someone brought a bear roast, the Chief said, "we cannot eat the bear meat." Two days prior to their arrival they did the Bear Dance, so the roast was removed, but the other food was okay.

The drumming got louder and they danced the Circle Dance. They asked us to join them and we both did. The following morning, they would ride to Cascade to the next campsite. The young runners would run a relay all the way as they had already run 700 miles or more from Northern Manitoba.

The Chief asked Meredith if she would ride his horse to White Hall Road, which was three miles, and she agreed. They formed a circle with all of the men sitting on the ground, crossing their legs. The Chief asked me to join them, so I did. They passed the Peace Pipe around and we all smoked from it.

The "staff" was then lifted up and the lead rider held it as they rode off. I told Meredith I would meet her at the railroad tracks on White Hall Road. The riders arrived at that destination point, but there was no one to replace Meredith. She looked down at me. "I'll meet you at Cascade," she said, and they rode off.

I got to Cascade and waited. They were coming at a gallop, rode in, and formed a circle. They continued to ride around and around, then the "staff" was once again placed in the ground. Meredith dismounted and I could immediately see that she was very sore (I don't believe she had been on a horse in years). I helped her to the van, where she told me that they had stopped at Billings and were fed food and Saskatoon berries. After that, they rode down the hill into Cascade; it was pouring rain and the horses had come on a dead run.

I finally got her home, poor little thing. She was only four foot, eleven and three quarters of an inch tall and only 100 lbs. She was so sore that she went straight to bed. After a couple of days, she was able to recuperate from her experience with the Metis Unity Ride.

When the Chief and I had sat in the yard visiting, he turned and looked at me and said, "Ron, this is a good place to be." It was a wonderful experience having them there for three days. The Unity Ride and Run was created to join people together. The drumming, dancing and singing were great! Meredith and I were very fortunate to have had them in our yard as our guests. I will never forget this!

CHAPTER THIRTY-EIGHT

SONS & GRANDSONS

Jesse and James grew into fine young men, both hard workers. James has his love, Kelsey, while Jesse dates and has a girlfriend. I'm very proud of both of them. They are extremely intelligent and I see a lot of Meredith in them. They can outwork anyone at a ratio of two to one. They get their endurance and strength from both of us. Jesse has helped me draft out a few of my inventions. Meredith has helped me draft some as well.

Over the years, Meredith helped me send out hundreds of lyrics. I even had my picture in a Nashville Newspaper as an up-and-coming writer. I had a few demos made. Meredith typed out one hundred of my poems, to compile into a book, which I wrote and have a copyright on. It's called "Old Dust".

I had to stop writing lyrics and poems when my priorities changed, having to take care of my wife and children.

My son, James and his lady Kelsey eventually had a baby. Seth Ritco, was born, a beautiful boy.

James was a firefighter, working for various companies, and eventually becoming an Initial Attack Crew Leader for the B.C. Forest Service. He continued upgrading his skills and knowledge and he has certificates of many kinds and levels.

I could always tell that James loves Kelsey with all of his heart, and she loves him back just as much. It makes my heart full when I see them with their children, building their life together. It reminds me of James' mom and I throughout our lives together, making me a proud father and grandfather. After they had been together for 15 years, they decided to get married. They got all dressed up for their day: a suit for James and a wedding gown for Kelsey. They took pictures in the back yard and other places as well, and went to the hot springs where they got married by the Justice of the Peace.

Being the grandpa, I looked after Harlen and Seth until they returned from their wedding and honeymoon.

Kelsey is a great mother. She takes loving care of her two sons and James. They raise the boys in a great way, giving them household chores and responsibilities, and they help their dad with outside work mowing lawns, raking, and getting firewood on the porch.

One fall, Jesse, James, Dale (Kelsey's dad), the two boys and I went hunting for moose, elk, deer, and grouse. We took a trailer up to Boundary Creek. Harlen and Seth learned gun safety and were good shots with a .22 caliber rifle. Both Harlen and Seth shot grouse, but Harlen managed to tally more than his brother.

Being an excellent cook, Kelsey had a wonderful recipe for grouse that makes your mouth water. Her sister and mom and her often get together to cook a batch of excellent Russian borscht. In the summer when we go camping, Kelsey, Kate, and their mother, Deb prepare wonderful meals, the kind of meals I've never seen before, and so delicious!

I am very fortunate to have in-laws of such a special caliber. Dale's a hunter, fisherman, and woodcutter. He is a hardworking man, we enjoy a lot of the same things, and I truly enjoy his company.

Huckleberry picking is enjoyed by the whole family, especially Kelsey, Deb and Kate's huckleberry tarts. Kate's husband is a great guy and is hospitable, kind and a good provider to his family. Kate and Luke have two daughters and I find them so humorous; as little people, they are completely genuine.

James and Kelsey are raising Harlen and Seth in a loving home and guiding them through life in a positive way. Harlen is an A and B student and Seth is a B and C+ student. From my perspective, I see only a good life for all of them and I love them all dearly.

CHAPTER THIRTY-NINE

JESSE

My first born, Jesse, is a great son. He went to college to become a mechanic, and has worked for various companies. Jesse and I would go up the North Fork Road, hunting, and come home with firewood to sell. We went camping at Marshall Lake last September and did some fishing as well, a great time for both of us. I brought my dog, Rudy with us. Rudy is a spirit dog and has a great sense of humor. While camping, he went to the next person's campground, stole their socks that were drying, and brought them to us. Jesse returned the socks and the campers just laughed.

Jesse dated different ladies for a few years. Jesse and Rosie started dating and had a baby, Milo. Jesse and Rosie's relationship ended, but Jesse sees Milo often and is very much a part of his life.

Jesse bought a house and started seeing a lady named Nicki. I could see that they loved each other and I hoped things would go well for both of them. Nicki got pregnant and in August, they got married in their backyard. I got to meet her mom, her dad, and her sister. I sensed they are good people as Nicki is a good person as a result of her mom and dad raising her with great qualities.

Jesse and Nicki had a son; they named him William. A few months later Nicki was pregnant with their second child. William was seven months old when he passed away. All of us were completely heartbroken. Jesse's friend, Mr. Harvey, his son, Jesse, and I built a coffin for little William. It was a very sad time for everyone. There are no words to express the loss we all felt. Nicki's mom and dad and their daughter's four children came from Edmonton (the mother of the four children was already here staying with Jesse and Nicki and looking for work). Family arrived from near and far. Simon Shenstone officiated the funeral service and did an excellent job as always. Nicki's dad and I were William's pallbearers. William is buried with my dad: Jesse's grandfather and William's great-grandfather.

The sadness of our loss of William is still with us. The loss of a child is unbearable. Nicki and Jesse now have a new son. His name is Nicolai, and he is a beautiful grandson, we all cherish him! Life goes on, but not without tears of the loss of William, may that little boy rest in peace.

Last fall, Jesse, James and I went hunting a few times. I took Harlen hunting up in the Blueberry/Paulson area. On the way up, Harlen shot a nice blue grouse. I wasn't able to call a moose in, unfortunately. Harlen set up a target and was shooting at 100 feet. He shot standing up and hit the three inch bullseye almost every time!

CHAPTER FORTY

CANCER

We found out Meredith had gotten lung cancer. One doctor told us she had arthritis, but no tests were done. Another doctor said the same and gave her a prescription for more pain medication.Then Dr. Ajero immediately sent her for X-rays and a test in Trail and at the Kelowna Hospital.

My brother George came and helped us as best as he could and after awhile, returned home. First they gave us hope, then they couldn't operate, then they could, and then they couldn't. At the end, they said she had three months to live.

Meredith's family came and we researched a variety of possible cures. Everyone left, but Meredith's sister Sandy came again and helped to make her comfortable as best we could. Again, we tried all kinds of possible cures. When Sandy left, Meredith could no longer take the pain and had no relief. I felt so helpless, there was nothing more I could do.

I called an ambulance and she was taken to the Grand Forks Hospital. They gave her pain medication via intravenous, and the family was notified and on their way, but the phone rang, and the hospital told me she was gone. My son Jesse and I went to the hospital, walked into her room, and our hearts shattered. Meredith's family came and I told them that her funeral would be held in our back yard. Everyone pitched in and we had her funeral.

My brother's daughter Virginia came, as well as a few friends of the kids and a few others, some of the members of the Metis Association, and of course all of the family. Meredith was cremated, her urn arrived, and the funeral began.

After everyone left, I covered the yard with my constant tears. My house caught on fire, but I kept the it at bay with a garden hose. until the fire department came. The insurance company did the repairs, so I decided to upgrade two bedrooms and the basement, needing something to take my mind off of my grief and sadness.

I moved down the hall to the end bedroom. The bed is facing north and my companions are Meredith's dog Rudy and her black footed African kitty, Sadie.

GOD HAS TAKEN MEREDITH HOME

CHAPTER FORTY-ONE

THREE MONTHS PASS

I was asleep in my bedroom when I heard her voice. "Ron, wake up." Quiet at first, then louder, "Ron wake up!" I woke out of a deep sleep. I was lying in bed with one arm under me slightly propped up. "It's not your time," I heard her say. I was in awe and did not reply, as I felt there was nothing I could say. I listened for the door to open or close, but there was no sound. I laid there until morning came, and, after getting up, looked through the room for speakers to explain what I had heard.

I called, Meredith's sister, Sandy that morning and told her what happened. The question was, *how can this happen?* Logic couldn't explain it. Is death another dimension that co-exists with life in a non-visible way? The first night she died, and Meredith was sent to the funeral home, they said they could not cremate her for thirty-six hours after her death. I was in bed, feeling relaxed, and started looking for her in my mind's eye. The vision that came to me that first night was: I saw a road or pathway. There were people walking in a slight uphill direction, three of them side by side. They were all wearing white gowns with a raised frill around the low-cut neck area, all dressed exactly the same. Meredith stopped, turned, and looked at me. She was absolutely beautiful, she was at peace, and she was going toward the light. My heart broke and swelled at the same time.

In another vision, I saw Meredith in the future. She was a captain on some type of spaceship, but she was taller, about five foot seven and so entrancing. I saw myself, also taller, walking on a bridge. She was so gorgeous and I knew that I loved her in this vision, but I was a cadet some sort of lower rank than she.

CHAPTER FORTY-TWO

DRIVING

A year after I lost my wonderful wife, I decided to go on a holiday. Meredith and I had talked about it before she passed away, and I thought it was finally time, so in mid-February, I got my passport and $3,500.00 U.S. Dollars, and jumped in the car.

I drove to Creston, stayed with my sister Robin, then to Sparwood to my cousin, Phillip and his wife, Brenda's place, then off to the border crossing south of Lethbridge, Alberta and into Montana. I spent two nights in Shelby, Montana. Outside the motel is a smoking room, and I was having a smoke when a man came in. He had a six-pack of beer and he offered me one. I took it and thanked him. I said, "I'm Ron Ritco from Grand Forks, British Columbia."

He laughed and said, "I'm Bill, from Grand Forks, North Dakota." We just laughed and drank our beer and he told me he worked in the oil fields.

The next day I went down to the gas station and there were two young people sitting on the sidewalk. I asked them if they were hitchhiking. "Heck no," the young man said. "See those trains down there? In a while they'll start moving west, that's when me and my girlfriend will jump on." They looked hungry, so I gave them twenty dollars to buy some food, and they thanked me. I went back to the motel; there were a few slot machines there, so I drank some beer and won a hundred and fifty dollars.

The next morning, I left, heading east. I stopped at different towns and checked out the thrift stores and secondhand stores, looking for antiques and collectibles. Old habits are hard to break. I stopped at every *Point of Interest* sign, thoroughly enjoying the legends and stories written on the signs; stories of days gone by that were wondrous and sad and true.

I found myself at, "The Rock," a marking stone from a river crossing. I walked up to it and felt something unexplainable. My eyes filled with tears and I could feel heartache and sadness. I went back to my car and brought some strands of Meredith's hair to place them in the earth beneath the stone. I gave tobacco to the earth, took a picture of the rock, then got back in my car and drove off.

The natives crossed the river where that rock was for many years, until the settlers moved the rock to a park. Eventually the native people got it back and they placed it on the side of Highway #2 in Montana, where it remains.

Driving south on Highway #85 through North Dakota and into South Dakota, I stopped and stayed at Hill City, and checked out the Dinosaur Museum and the Rock Shop. I stopped at Crazy Horse's monument and watched a film showing the great feat of carving the monument. I was the only person in the theater. They drove me to the bottom of the monument. I got out and let loose a few strands of Meredith's hair, and they gently blew in the wind. I then crushed some sweet grass and let it fall to the ground. The bus driver drove me back to the museum of indian artifacts. Again, I was the only person on the bus. After spending six hours at the museum, I rolled one strand of Meredith's hair and placed it outside of the building.

From there, I drove to Mount Rushmore, then the Mammoth Dig, where I enjoyed another tour. At one of the dig sites, there was an archeologist, working away. Looking through the ground in front of her, I could see a young man who wasn't there. I said, "keep digging, I think you will find a young man ahead of

you." She laughed and shook her head. That evening, I had dinner in the restaurant near the dig site. The same lady and her friend were also there. As I was leaving and walking past their table, she recognized me from earlier.

"Do you really think there is a human being buried there?" she asked.

"Yes, I see a person there." I don't know if they found the body, but I knew that it was a boy of fourteen years that I had visualized.

I arrived at Bell ha Faunch and was getting gas, and I could see that they had a few slot machines inside the station. I asked the clerk if there was a large casino nearby. "You want to go to Deadwood," she responded. I continued driving until I reached Deadwood an hour later. I found an affordable place to stay; there was an antique store as well and I bought a few things. Up the road was another place with antiques, and I bought a few things there as well. Back in Deadwood, there was a little old lady who worked at the tourist information center. We visited for a bit and I found out that she collected Canadian coins. I told her I would find her a few antique ones and get them to her.

Deadwood was great: the old buildings, the gambling. I won and lost and laughed. Wild Bill Hickock and Calamity Jane once walked these streets and visited the hotels, days gone by. I promised myself I would return again. I headed off to Nebraska for breakfast because, why not? I was only sixty miles away. I visited Custer's battlefield, the historic place where Custer and his men fell to the Native warriors he could not beat.

Back on the road, I started heading north. Two or three days later, I arrived at Laurier Customs. It was 11:00 p.m. I visited with the Customs Officer as she enjoyed historic sites, and I told her of everything that I had seen. After enjoying the three-thousand mile drive I had been on, I was fourteen miles from home and all was well.

The following year I went for another drive, this time with my sister, Robin, and my brother, George. We stayed in different towns and visited Chief Joseph's battlefield and, "The Devil's Tower." We spent the night fifty miles down the road in a place called Gilette. George wanted to take a different route to go to Custer's Last Stand battlefield, so we decided to explore. Ten hours later, we wound up forty miles from where we had originally stayed in Gilette. We had just driven three hundred miles in a circle. We couldn't help but laugh when we realized it.

After that, we drove to Billings, Montana. We spent a few nights along the way, then headed north to Creston, British Columbia. While in Deadwood, I left some Canadian coins for the lady who worked at the Information Center. She wasn't there that day, but her co-worker said she would make sure she got the coins. A week later, the little old lady phoned me and thanked me for the coins. She wanted to pay me for them, but I told her that they were a gift, so I couldn't take any money.

CHAPTER FORTY-THREE

THE WHITE RAT

In another one of my vivid dreams, I could see a person's neck. I couldn't see the head or below the shoulders. A white rat comes out of the shirt and climbs onto the shoulder of that person. This dream occurred three nights in a row.

A couple of weeks later, I was out working, having just finished installing an underground sprinkler system for Mrs. Summerland. I drove down her driveway and went through the open gate. I stopped and closed the large steel gate, got back into my car, and looked to my left for any traffic. No one was coming, so I pulled out and turned right. As I was turning, I looked across the road and could see a young man wearing an Indiana Jones style hat walking in the opposite direction. It looked as if he'd had a hard time recently, so stopped on the side of the road and called him over.

I gave him twenty dollars and told him to get some food. As he reached out and took the money, he said, "Thank you, it's my birthday, I'm twenty years old today." As he smiled, his shirt started moving and a white rat came out and sat on his shoulder.

I laughed wished him a happy birthday. When he saw me looking at the rat, he said, "This is my pet rat. He's travelling with me." I haven't seen the young man since, but have not forgotten my dream and the day I met the white rat.

CHAPTER FORTY-FOUR

A MOMENT OF WORRY

One morning in 2013, I found a small growth on my ear; it hurts and was burning. I went to a doctor and he burned it off with nitric acid. A week later, it was back. Again, the doctor burned it off. After another week, it came back and doctor decided to cut it out. A week after that, it returned again and my ear turned red, burning with a constant pain, reminding me of a wasp sting.

I decided to go on an alkaline diet and take various vitamins and minerals. I also started taking D.C.A. as well. I had bought it for my wife's cancer, but before she had a chance to take it, she passed away. I started meditating and would visualize an army of Vikings running through my veins, hunting the cancer with the intent to eradicate it with their axes and spears. I listened to Credence Clearwater Revival and Beethoven.

Two weeks passed, and the burning sensation was gone. I went back to my normal diet, happy that I was still alive. What awaits me in the near future I do not know, and don't want to know. Que Sur Ra, Sur Ra, whatever will be, will be!!!

CHAPTER FORTY-FIVE

LIFE CONTINUES ON

Our cat Sadie passed away on November 21st, 2015. I baptized her and asked her to give my Meredith a kiss on the cheek and tell her I love her. Meredith had been gone for four years, and my heart was still broken. I buried Sadie in the backyard.

Nicki's mom and dad moved to Grand Forks and were staying with Jesse and Nicki. I took Nicki's dad,

James, out hunting. We went up the North Fork Road, over 28-Mile Bridge, onto Granby Road, crossed Cable Creek, then Uno Creek, down the Boundary Creek, and finally onto West Fork. We stopped and saw some moose tracks and a fresh bear track.

We drove down Sebastian Creek Road, stopped at a good spot, and got out of the truck. I did a moose call and suddenly a wolf howled a hundred fifty yards away from us. I did another more moose call and a pack of wolves answered. I suggested to James that we get out of there, since the wolves seemed very interested in us. I drove down Sebastian Road and we stopped at Williamson Lake. I made some coffee and we tried fishing, but didn't catch anything, so we left and drove down Sebastian onto Christian Valley Road, to West Bridge, Rock Creek, Midway, and Greenwood, then back home to Grand Forks. It was a great day; James got to see some of the area and we got to visit and get to know each other even better.

The next season, Jesse, James, and myself entered the limited hunting draw for the area. We got two bull-moose tags and three cow-elk tags. We set out and camped on Boundary Creek. We had a friend, Dale Day, as well as Seth and Harlen along for the trip. We spent long, hard days hunting and managed to get two moose, one dressed out at 340 lbs. and one at 540 lbs. We had to go out and buy another freezer just for the meat.

We then went out elk hunting; Jesse and Dale chased an elk for nine miles and got it. James and I were wondering where they were, but they eventually showed up with their elk. James and Dale got another elk, and James and I both got a Spike white-tailed deer. Harlen even got a grouse. All of the success, not to mention the cribbage games made that a hunting season to remember.

CHAPTER FORTY-SIX

MY INVENTIONS

The following are a few of the inventions I've come up with over the years:

- A new way of rebuilding the spine (rough schematics were sent to Christopher Reid and The Man in Motion).
- A way of making a river in the southern states (schematics were sent to Governor Arnold Schwarzenegger) this would be a new supply of fresh water.
- A way of diverting water from Winnipeg to avoid floods in the city.
- A project called Olympian Train (transportation from Washington State to Southern California).
- A hydrogen water separator system which also generates electricity with a cooling condenser to lower the temperature in the Gulf by two degrees or more to subdue the creation of hurricanes.

My friend Dave Brummett helped me and worked with me on some of these projects:

- We came up with fourteen different ways of stopping the oil flow into the Gulf. Copies were sent out to the Governor of Louisiana, Texas, and another coastal state. One copy was sent to the P.M. Of Great Britain; One copy was sent to Deep Horizon Response; and I think one copy was sent to the U.S. President. These inventions are not designed to make money; this was a gift to the world. We have received a letter of thanks from Great Britain and one of the three U.S. States that we had mailed a copy to.
- Dave and I also drafted up the Crash and Terrorist Proof Plane. A disclosure was sent to Boeing and Bombardier. No response has been received to date.
- My son, Jesse, helped me draft up plans for the ultimate tire. No response has been received to date.

I have inserted some of my sketches, letters and descriptions in the following pages. My hope is to invent something good in the future. This is my journey through life.

Please Note When you have a family
Of 5 children and somtimes
2 more which are foster children
and you have a Lady to Love

We could not aford a copie write cost
as it was $25.00 Per song
so I would mail it to myself.
For Protections

Ron Ritco & Dave Brummet,
121 Sagamore Ave.,
Grand Forks, B.C.,
V0H 1H4, Canada.
Ph. # 250-442-0867/250-442-4218
Email: sadie48@telus.net
May 07,2010.

To: Whom It May Concern

Re: Solving the oil leak and oil slick in the Gulf of Mexico.

Dear Sir or Madam,

My name is Ron Ritco, and my Partner Dave Brummet and I would like to submit the enclosed schematics, of which we are the inventors, for two devices that we believe will contain the oil well leak in the Gulf of Mexico.

The first is called a "Bungbrella" and the second is a "Wellveil", which will solve the problem of the oil that is spilling into the ocean.

As well, we have experimented with Roxul insulation, which absorbs the surface oil and which could be used for cleanup of surface oil slick, because of it's absorbency.

We can be reached at the above email address or by phone for more detailed info if needed.

Hope that you will take this seriously.

Thank you for your prompt attention.

Sincerely,

Ron Ritco, Dave Brummet.

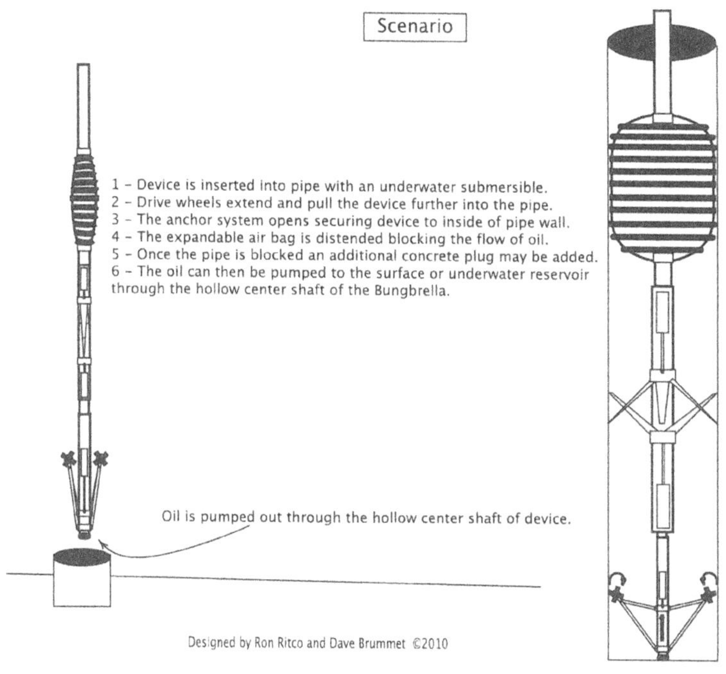
Scenario
1 - Device is inserted into pipe with an underwater submersible.
2 - Drive wheels extend and pull the device further into the pipe.
3 - The anchor system opens securing device to inside of pipe wall.
4 - The expandable air bag is distended blocking the flow of oil.
5 - Once the pipe is blocked an additional concrete plug may be added.
6 - The oil can then be pumped to the surface or underwater reservoir through the hollow center shaft of the Bungbrella.
Oil is pumped out through the hollow center shaft of device.
Designed by Ron Ritco and Dave Brummet ©2010

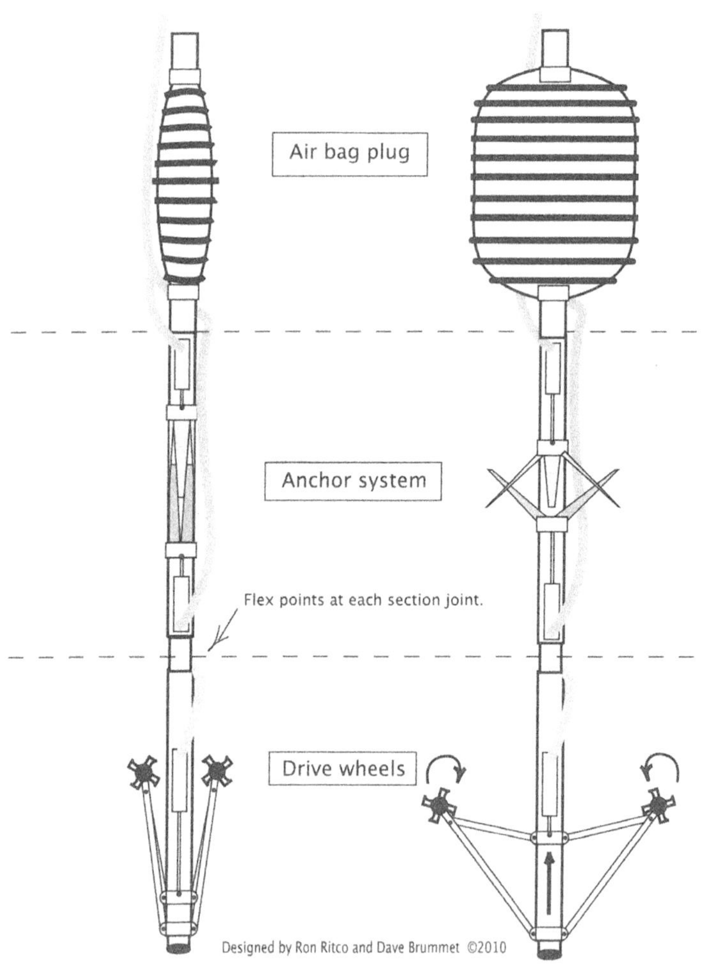
Air bag plug
Anchor system
Flex points at each section joint.
Drive wheels
Designed by Ron Ritco and Dave Brummet ©2010

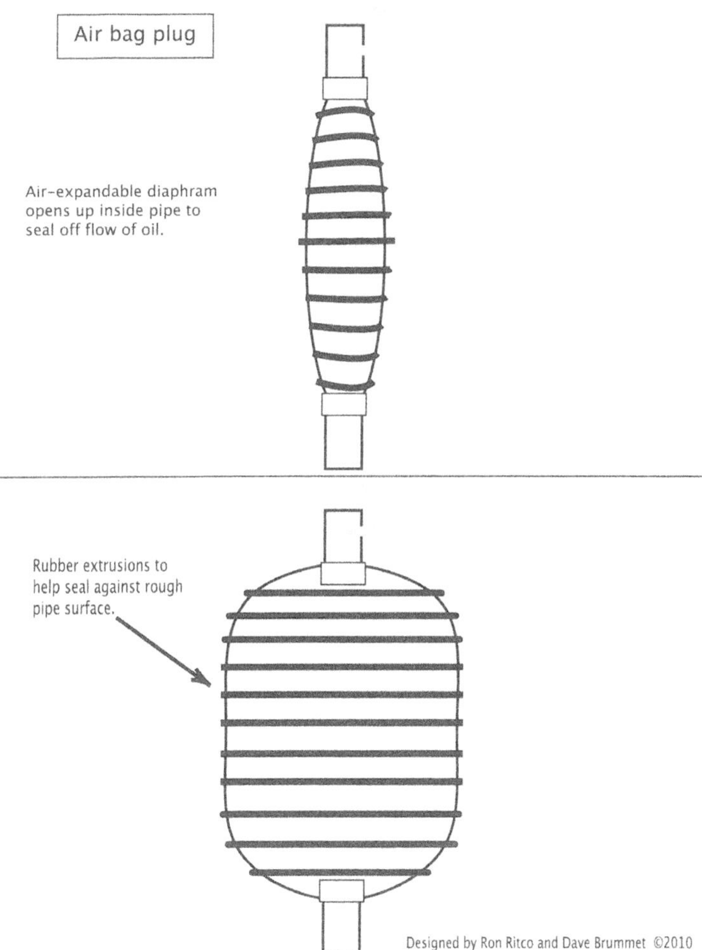
Air bag plug
Air-expandable diaphram opens up inside pipe to seal off flow of oil.
Rubber extrusions to help seal against rough pipe surface.
Designed by Ron Ritco and Dave Brummet ©2010

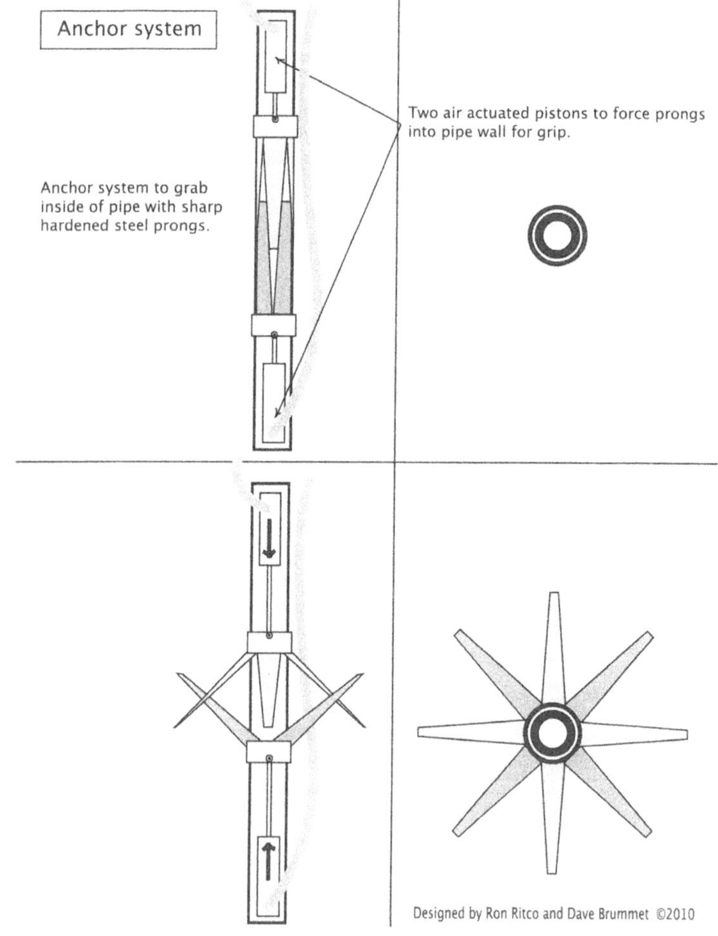
Anchor system
Two air actuated pistons to force prongs into pipe wall for grip.
Anchor system to grab inside of pipe with sharp hardened steel prongs.
Designed by Ron Ritco and Dave Brummet ©2010

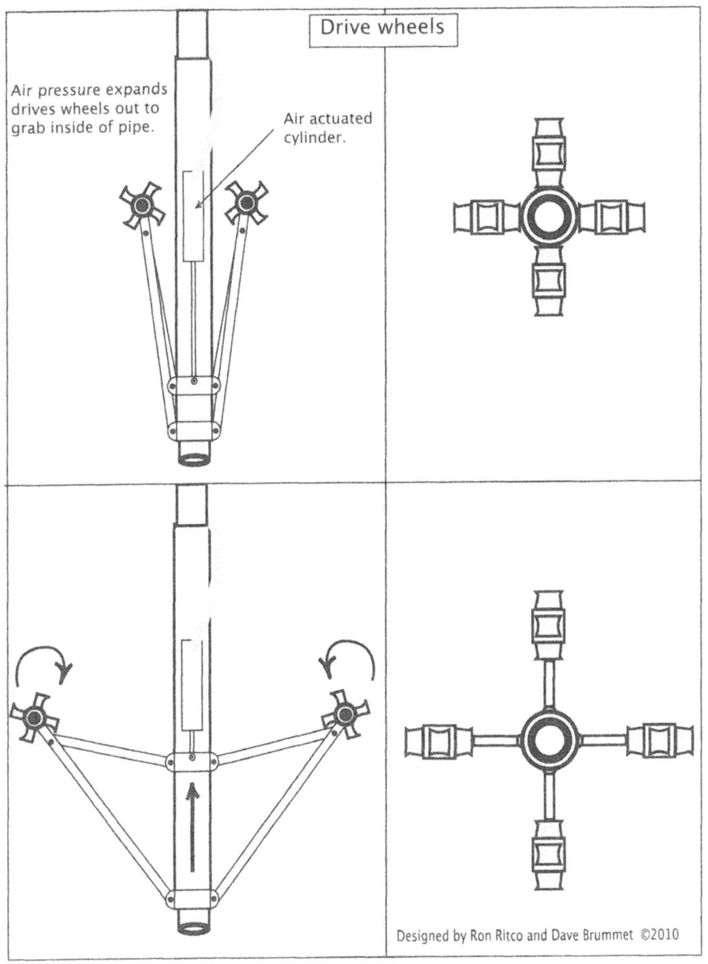
Drive wheels
Air pressure expands drives wheels out to grab inside of pipe.
Air actuated cylinder.
Designed by Ron Ritco and Dave Brummet ©2010

WellVeil can be shipped in folded map-like configuration. When unfurled vertically air pressure injected at bottom of veil will help open up the membrane quicker. Crossbracing ensures veil will hold shape in currents. Pool installed at top is like a kiddie pool - inflatable sides for support and in conjunction with the pontoons it will aid in keeping the veil buoyant.
Veil can be used along with Bungbrella to help contain any oil missed by sump system. Could be readily installed on all ocean rigs for instant retrieval and minimum environmental damage.

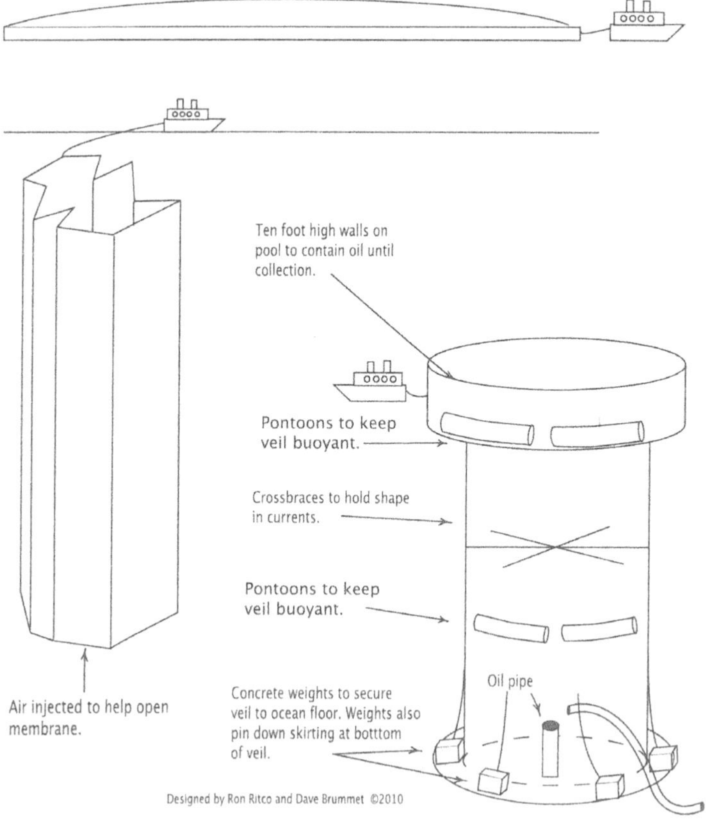

Gary D. Warden
Engineer

BP Crisis & Continuity Management
Oil Spill Technology
501 Westlake Park Blvd, Houston, TX 77079

Tel: (281) 566-2000
Email: Gary.Warden@bp.com

January 8, 2013

Ron Ritco
121 Sagamore Avenue
Grand Forks, BC, Canada
V0H 1H4
+1 (250) 442-0867

New Invention/Design/Idea to Seal Wellhead in the Gulf of Mexico

Dear Ron Ritco:

I am writing in response to your March 26, 2012 letter addressed to BP's CEO and Board of Directors in which you and your co-inventor (Dave Brummet) offered BP an opportunity to review documentation of your new invention/design/idea for sealing the wellhead in the Gulf of Mexico if BP agrees to your non-disclosure agreement. First, please accept my apology for the lengthy delay in my reply to your offer.

BP is very appreciative of the many thousands of people across the globe who offered their ideas for stopping the flow of oil into the Gulf and for containing the oil. People from over 100 different countries suggested over 100,000 ideas for stopping the flow of oil in the Gulf of Mexico or containing the spill. Many of the ideas received were very similar to each other, including many that duplicated or were similar to our own internal ideas and developments.

We have searched our Alternative Response Technology (ART) databases where ideas submitted during Deepwater Horizon (DWH) are stored and failed to find any submitted by Dave Brummet or yourself. We did however find approximately 20 very similar ideas using a spear like device with an expandable bladder or umbrella that could be deployed by injecting either air or inert gas. In each case the idea was judged by the Screening Team to be unfeasible in the extreme conditions that existed in the DWH well.

Building on the lessons learned during the DWH incident, BP has developed what we think is the best well capping system in the industry. Capping and Containment capabilities have also advanced significantly within industry organizations like the Marine Well Containment Company (MWCC) and OGP's Subsea Well Response Project (SWRP). In light of these advances BP has taken the position that we will support the development of additional capping and containment options through industry organizations. Accordingly BP will decline your offer to review documentation on your new invention, however it may be appropriate for you to share your offer with organizations like MWCC and SWRP, both of which BP supports.

We truly appreciate you taking the time and effort to offer BP the opportunity to review your new idea; thank you for your interest in oil spill prevention and response technology.

Sincerely,

Gary D. Warden

Gary D. Warden
BP Crisis & Continuity Management – Oil Spill Technology

10 DOWNING STREET
LONDON SW1A 2AA
www.number10.gov.uk

From the Direct Communications Unit

12 July 2010

Mr Dave Brrummet
121 Sagmore Avenue
Grand Forks
British Columbia
Canada
V0H 1H4

Dear Mr Brrummet

I am writing on behalf of the Prime Minister to thank you and Mr Ron Ritco for your letter of 7 May.

It is good of you to get in touch. Mr Cameron very much appreciates your taking the time and trouble to inform him of your views.

With best wishes.

Yours sincerely

S Caine

MR S CAINE

HM TREASURY Spending Challenge

The Spending Challenge is your chance to shape the way Government works, and help us get more for less as we try to bring down the deficit. Please visit **www.hm-treasury.gov.uk/spendingchallenge** from 9 July to share your suggestions.

STATE OF FLORIDA
Office of the Governor
THE CAPITOL
TALLAHASSEE, FLORIDA 32399-0001

www.flgov.com
850-488-4441
850-487-0801 fax

CHARLIE CRIST
GOVERNOR

May 28, 2010

Mr. Ron Ritco
121 Sagamore Avenue
Grand Forks, British Columbia
V0H 1H4
CANADA

Dear Mr. Ritco:

Thank you for contacting Governor Charlie Crist and sharing your concerns about the oil spill in the Gulf of Mexico. Governor Crist asked that I respond on his behalf.

On Tuesday, April 20, 2010, an offshore oil drilling platform, Deepwater Horizon, exploded in the Gulf of Mexico near Louisiana. Tragically, 11 men lost their lives in the blast. The oil well was owned by BP, while the rig was owned by Transocean Ltd and serviced by Halliburton. The rig is now submerged at the bottom of the Gulf. Under federal law, BP is the party responsible for cleanup operations.

According to estimates from the National Oceanic and Atmospheric Administration (NOAA), the rig was discharging at least 5,000 barrels of oil (210,000 gallons) per day. BP was able to insert a device into the largest breach which greatly reduced, but not eliminated, the amount of oil and gas spewing into the Gulf.

On April 27, Governor Crist was among the first to fly over the oil slick to gauge its threat to Florida's coastline and small businesses along the Gulf Coast. From the early days following the explosion and oil discharges, Governor Crist has taken action to ensure that Florida's beaches and affected industries are protected. The Governor has personally led Florida's efforts to work with federal, state, and local authorities to put the well-being of both residents and visitors at the top of the list.

Governor Crist has taken these specific actions:

- Declared a State of Emergency on April 30 for several Gulf Coast counties to protect the citizens, visitors, natural resources and businesses. This action also eased the coordination between the state and federal government as well as the state and local governments. This state of emergency exists for the following counties: Escambia, Santa Rosa, Okaloosa, Walton, Bay, Gulf, Franklin, Wakulla, Jefferson, Taylor, Dixie, Levy, Citrus, Hernando, Pasco, Pinellas, Hillsborough, Manatee, Sarasota, Charlotte, Lee, Collier, Monroe, Miami-Dade, Broward and Palm Beach.

- Designated David Halstead, Director of the Florida Division of Emergency Management as the State Coordinating Officer and directed him to activate the state's Comprehensive Emergency Management Plan and other response, recovery and mitigation plans necessary to cope with the emergency. This includes activation of the Florida National Guard for the duration of the emergency.

Mr. Ron Ritco
May 28, 2010
Page Two

- Designated the Florida Department of Environmental Protection (DEP) the lead state agency for responding to potential impacts of the oil spill along Florida's shoreline. For the latest news, answers to frequently asked questions and information about the oil spill's impact on vulnerable animal life and the seafood industry, please view the Department of Environmental Protection's Web site online at www.dep.state.fl.us/deepwaterhorizon/default.htm. For more information, you may wish to call the Florida State Emergency Information Line toll-free at (800) 342-3557.

- Visited the Apalachicola region, which is responsible for most of America's oyster production, on May 8. Governor Crist participated in oyster harvests and pledged the resources of Florida State government to protect the seafood industry, tourism and other vital lifeblood industries of the region.

- Joined with Attorney General Bill McCollum on May 10 to appoint former Attorneys General Bob Butterworth and Jim Smith to lead an oil incident legal advisory council. The advisory council will work to prepare Florida for any future litigation, enforcement, or regulatory action that may be needed against BP, Transocean and Halliburton. Those with questions about the Deepwater Horizon Oil Spill Legal Advisory Council should call the Attorney General's toll-free hotline at 1-866-966-7226.

- Created the Gulf Oil Spill Economic Recovery Task Force on May 11. This group, comprised of representatives from state and local governments, the hospitality industry and tourism industry, will monitor BP's efforts in providing financial relief to impacted businesses and ensure that the vitality of the business and tourism industries continue to prosper. To protect affected businesses, the Task Force will ensure economic loss data and industry economic indicators are effectively collected

- Called on BP to provide significant funding for a marketing campaign to counter negative and false information appearing in print and electronic media about the spill's impact on Florida's beaches and waters. On May 17, BP Chief Executive Officer Tony Hayward came to Tallahassee to inform the Governor, and the State of Florida, that BP would grant the Governor's request and provide $25 million for the marketing campaign.

Thank you again for taking the time to contact the Governor's Office and for sharing your concerns about this issue of national importance.

Sincerely,

Willem J. de Greef
Office of Citizen Services

WJDG/cas

Rick Hansen Man In Motion Foundation

5th Floor 520 West 6th ave
Vancover, B.C. Canada
V5Z-1A1

FAX-604-876-6666

SENT OUT Jan 5/2004

Ph 604-876-6800
604 822-4433

Feb. 11th phoned awaiting a response or email.

Ph. March 7 2006
asked if they have done anything with
this Idea.
waiting for a call back.

Also sent to Christopher Reed Society
No responses as yet.
Jan/5/2004

FAX

To: Rick Hansen
From: Ron Ritco
Name:
Date sent: Jan 5/04
Phone number:
Number of Pages: 20
Fax number: 604-876-6666

Message: Possible new system

Mr. Rick Hansen

I hope that there is
some potentail in what
I have sent you to resolve
the problem at hand

Ron Ritco

121 Sagamore Ave
Grand Forks B.C.
Can.
V0H-1H4
Ph. 442-0867

Project Oct 4th 2003
To date Jan 4th 2004

By Ron Ritco

P.1

Dear Sir:

The goal of this design, system is to:

1 Drill a hole in the existing bone

2 atach eyelets to the wall of the existing ~~boan~~ bone and to the shard that is putting Presure on~~e~~ the spinal cord.

3 Thread a wire through the eyelets with a magnetic tipped needle

4 Fracture the shard and pull the shard into the area, that the hole has drilled.

5 Fill the area with Plastic, wax? or eny safe media. redrill and pull again untill the Preasure on the spinal cord is releaved.

6 On a colapesed area

A a small drill hole is needed to Put a ~~x~~ hollow needle through the colapesed area.

B Now Fill the area as the needle is pulled out with Plastic or some high expantion material?

P. 2

C We need a base ~~to lay~~ or foundation to work from.

D We can continue with a material that has a expantion or ~~life~~ lift capability one layer ontop of another if this works.

E Or we now use a connected ~~on~~ line of blocks that are designed as to an exact degree of arch, So as not to travel into the spinal cord and not to travel outward.

F EACH one ~~will~~ line, of continuouse blocks, Will travel on the second, third, fourth ect. untill we have ~~a~~ replaced the colapsed area.

Layer upon Layer

G EACH block has an air Pin or air jack on each cornner

"If needed" we can now lift even more when one side or the other needs to be lifted to level the blocks. for the next layer?

P. 3

F The shape of each block "Slide"
• Must be the most realistic
shape that eliminates eny
slide problemes, or binding as
one layer slides on the second
ed.

G Once this bridge has been
built, we can fill and bind
each securly buy now filling
the air pin condlk with plastic?

DRILL BIT

(1)

DRIVE SHAFT

SURFACE AREA
OF HEAD 180°

INNER ROLLER

MOTOR

4 AIR DRIVE
WHEELS

IN/OUT AIR PRESS.

FORWARD/REVERS
AIR.

AIR ↑
ELEC.
IF USED

DRIVE MECHINISUM / 1

Page 2

1) DENTAL-Drill

2) ForWARD AND REVERS

3) DRIVE TUBE MUST NOW HAVE CONSISTANT CONNECTIONS w/ UNIVERSALES CONNECTED TO EACH other "INSIDE" OF A HOSE, BUT A AIR VACUM HOSE MUST BE BESIDE IT

NOW THE Drill CAN TurN

180°

PIVIT POINT

4) AIR PRESS

UP

DOW

DRILL HEAD FRONT OF DRILL

IN OR OUT AIR PRESSURE NOW AT Four Points AT THE BACK OF THE DRILL. STEARS THE DRILL IN ENY Direction AS AIR PRESSURE IN THE FOUR SLIDES REGULATE DIRECTION OF drill.

~~HEAD OF DRILL~~

AIRINTAKE

DIAFRAME

TO FORCE DRILL, TO DRILL LARGER HOLES WHEN AIR PRESSURE IS INCREASED ("IE" CORNERS)

1
3

COLAPES DISC + PRESSER ON SPINAL CORD

1/8" of

DRILL HOLE

SPINAL CORD

DISC

HOLE AREA MUST HOLD THE BONE
WHICH IS PRESSING ON SPINAL CORD

F

(FRACTURE POINTS)

~~OR IF NEEDED~~ - PULL THE BONE
INWARD - FILL HOLE with PLASTIC?
THEN REDRILL SECOND HOLE ECT

2 to 1 PULL RATIO

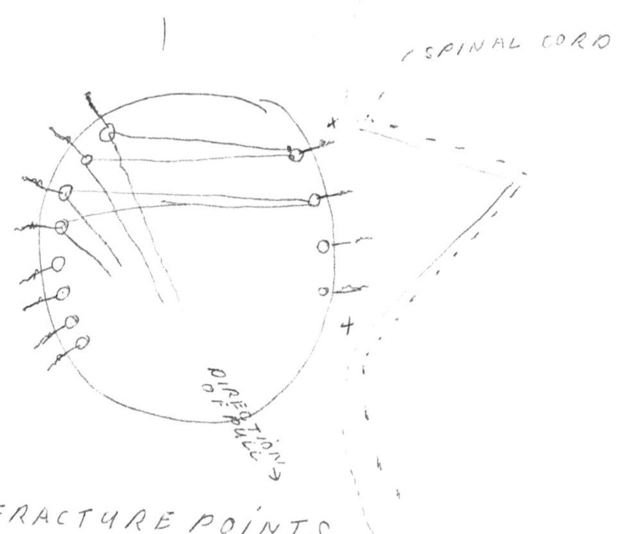

X = FRACTURE POINTS
VIA - LASER OR EXPLOSION

P.S. AN ENGENERR WILL GIVE
FORCE-RESISTANCE-EQUATION
AND LOCATION FOR (EYELETS)
+ PULL FORCE

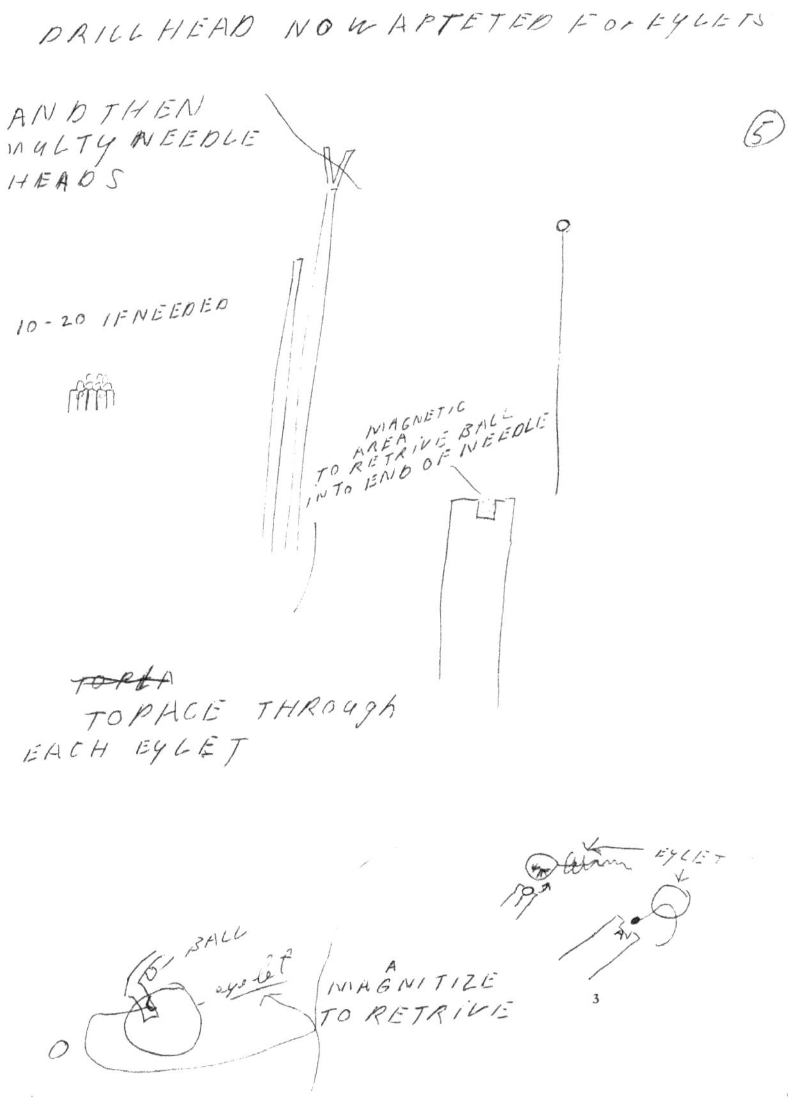

DRILL HEAD NOW APTETED FOR EYLETS

AND THEN
MULTY NEEDLE
HEADS

(5)

10-20 IF NEEDED

MAGNETIC
TO AREA
TO RETRIVE BALL
INTO END OF NEEDLE

~~TO PLA~~
TOPACE THROUGH
EACH EYLET

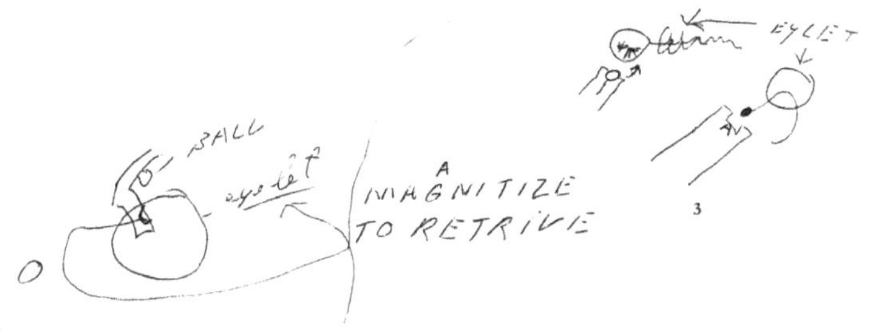

6

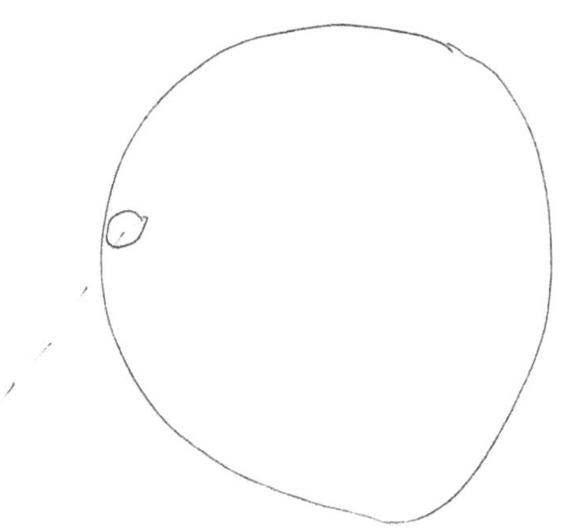

IF POSIBBLE ATUBE LEFT
BENIND TO REFILL HOLE IF
SECOND DRILL HOLE IS NEEDE

DEGRE OF ANGEL = DEGREE O SHAPE

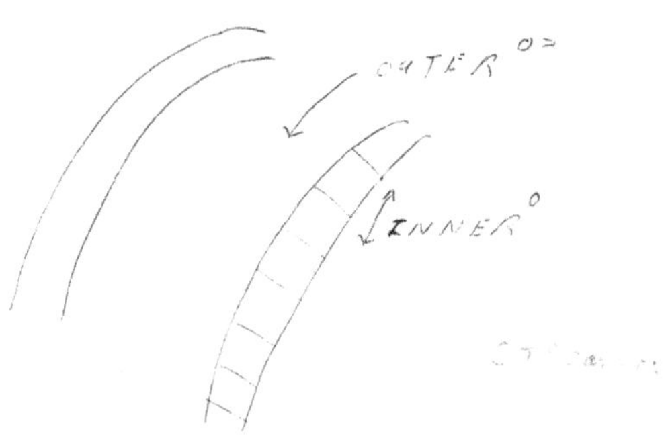

COLAPESED VERTIBRA

DRILL HEAD NOW DRILLS THIS SHAPE AND PULLS THIS SHAPE OF TRAIN CARS BEHIND IT THROUGH THIS AREA TO SOLID STRUCTURE OF BONE

~~DRILL H~~

SECOND DRILL PULLS NEXT LAYER ON TOP OF 1ST ECT UNTILL AREA IS REGAINED

Page 8

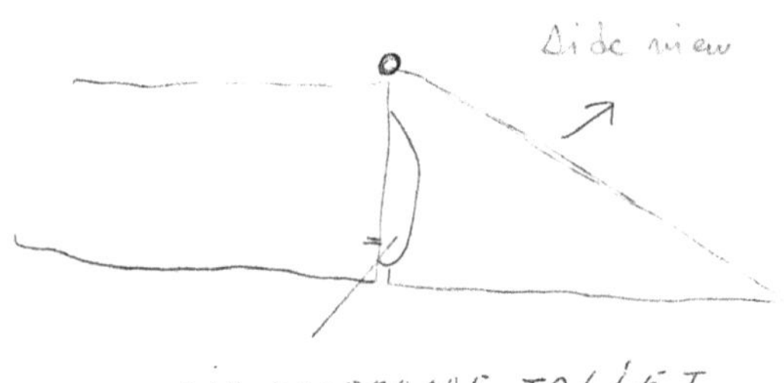

(1) AIR PIN
ON EACH SIDE OF TRAIN CAR

AIR
BLADER
air in

ONE WAY
VALVES

AIR →

THIS AIR PIN NOW EXPANDES
TO MAKE A PILLER TOLIFT
COLAPESED AREA
THIS IS NOW THE BEAM IN A BRIDGE
SECOND LAYER WILL LIFT (AGAIN)

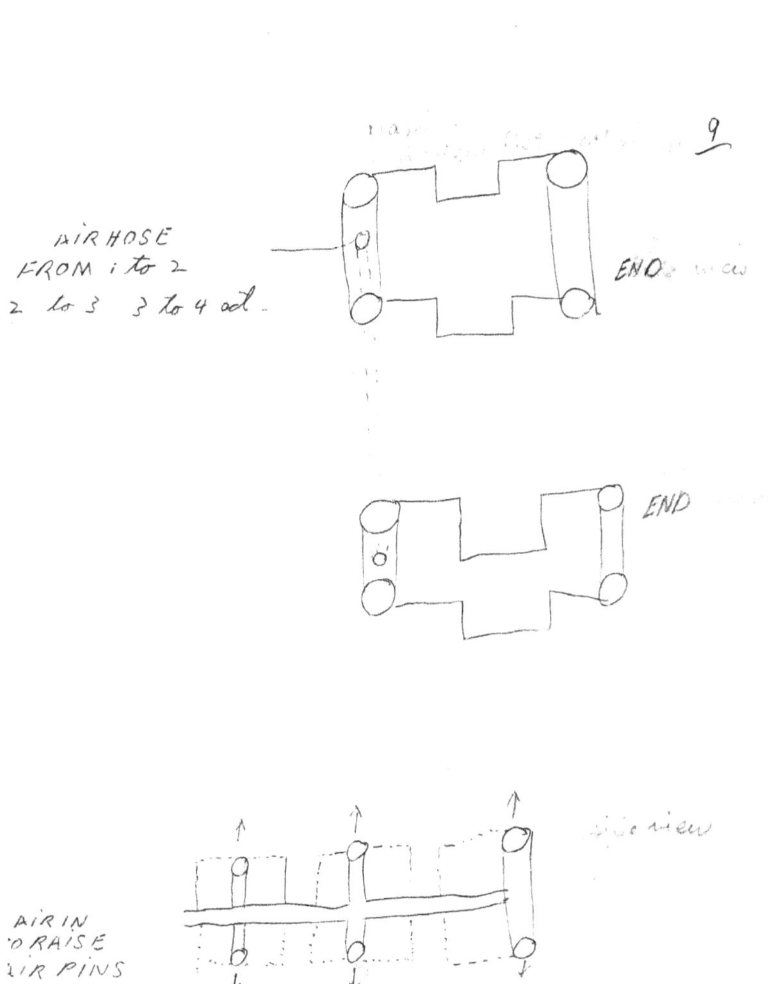
9
AIR HOSE
FROM 1 to 2
2 to 3 3 to 4
END
END
AIR IN
RAISE
PINS

"OPtion 2"

The object is to place a shield between the spinal cord and the area we will now fill with plastic expandable lift capabilities to rebuild colapsed area. Layer upon layer.

ORTION NO.2 Page (1)

HOLLOW NEDLE HEAD CARRIES LIQUID PLASTIC

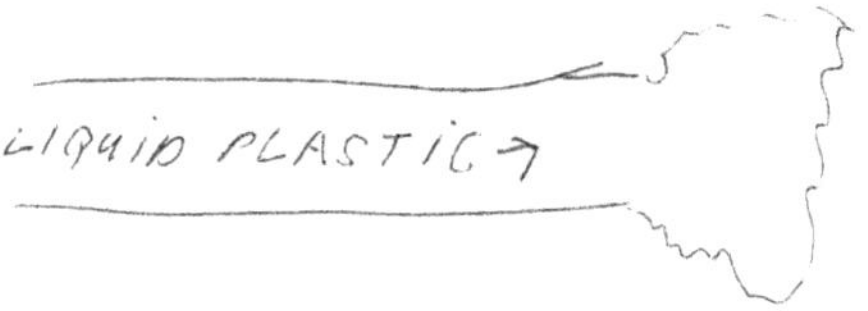

LIQUID PLASTIC →

arch = replacement shape.

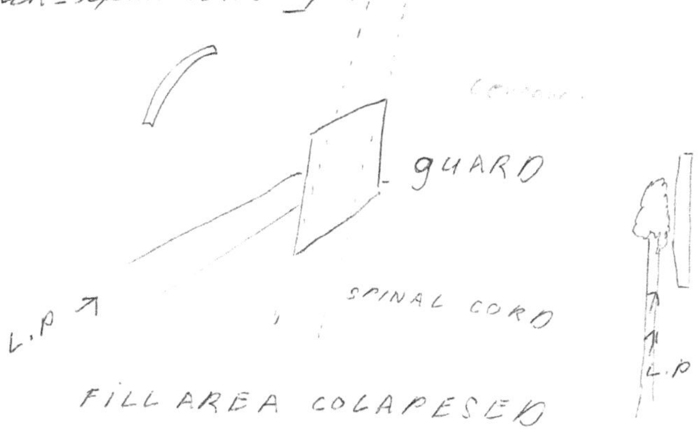

GUARD

L.P ↗

SPINAL CORD

L.P

FILL AREA COLAPESED

OPTION NO 2 — Page (2)

computer
/
Skeletal -

CONNECTOR GUARD 1 to 2/2 to 3 ect.

2 - 3 - 4 CONECTING POINTS ON EACH GUARD

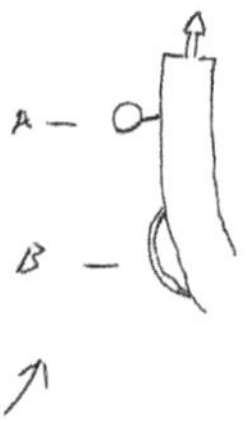

x + B are areas
n which the Plastic
an flow into.
o secure the plastic
to the sheild as rebar
is to cement

INNER ARCH = O

OUTER ARCH = O

O = EXACT ARCH NEEDED

OPTION 2 Page 3

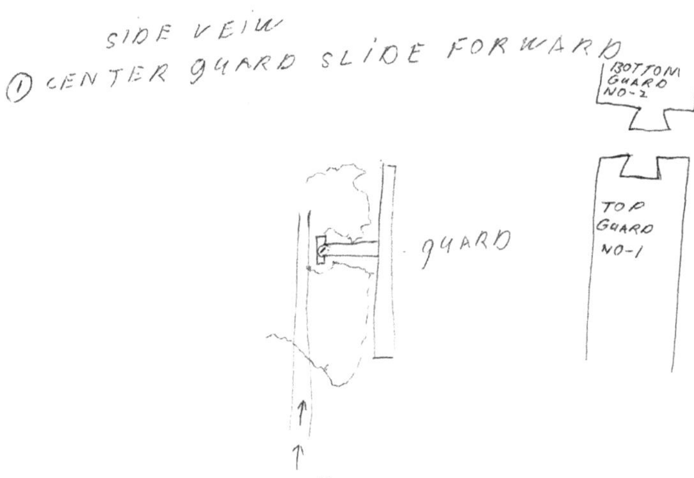

each guard has an exat degree of arch to steer the gaurd From Point A to Point B each guard is inter locked at top and bottom to interlock the first layer to the second to the third ect.

OPTION 3 P.1

AIR FILLED

PLASTIC FILLED

WIRE

RUBBER OUTER

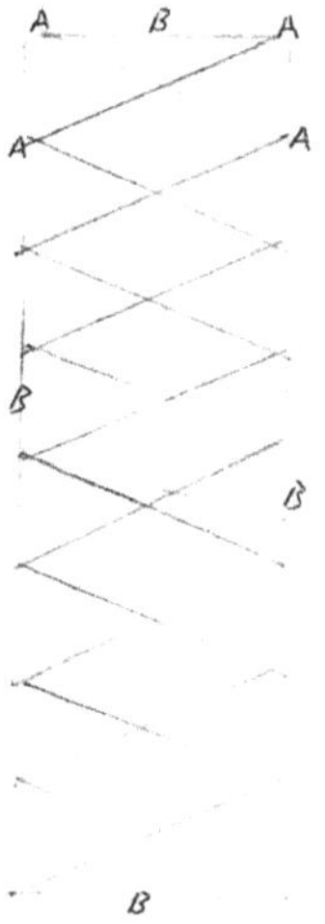

A B A

A A

B

B

B

END VIEW

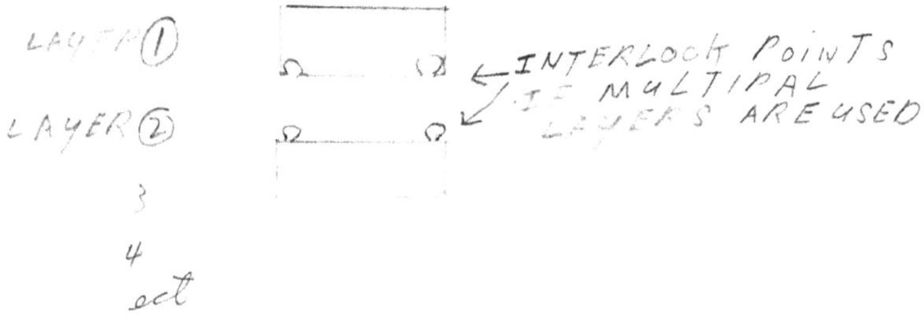

LAYER (1)

LAYER (2)

3

4

ect

INTERLOCK POINTS IF MULTIPAL LAYERS ARE USED

Option 3 P. 2

The outer weave will be large alowing the exterior shape to be greater than the interior weave to be finner as to keep the inner area around the spinal cord smaller.

This weave system when filled with air Or plastic will now lift and shape the area replacing the vertabra and protect the spinal cord.

This is baseactly a bag with wire weave to keep it in an exact shape when filled with air or plastic Pat.

P.S. SPIDER WEAVE MATEREAL is 100 x stronger than steel wire This gives the weave greater strength in less area

OP. 4 P. 2

2 - air Pins FROM TOP VERTABA
to BOTTEM VERTABA

AT OUTSIDE EDGE OF SPINAL CORD

ANOTHER SET ON OPPOSITE SIDE

FILL with AIR, PLASTIC, OR OTHER MEDIA
This will NOW LIFT SPIN BACK TO ORIGINAL
HEIGHT

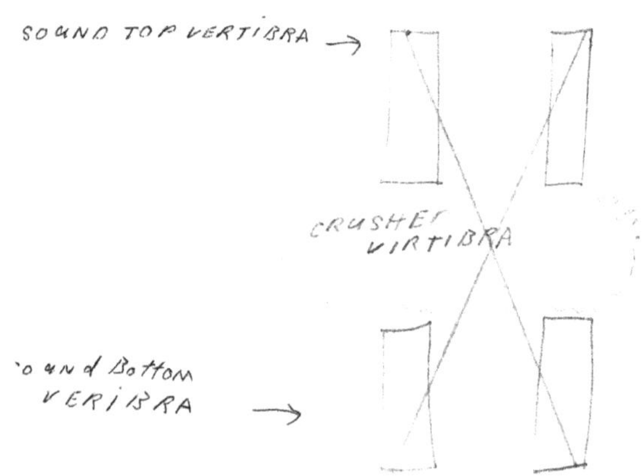

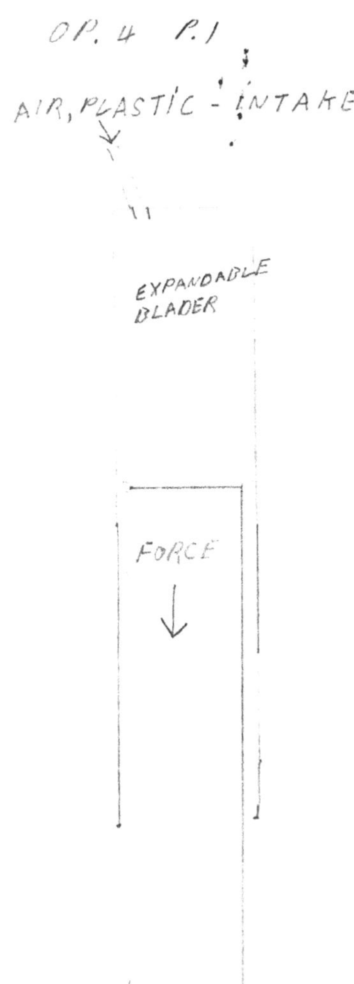
OP. 4 P. 1
AIR, PLASTIC - INTAKE
EXPANDABLE
BLADER
FORCE

GOVERNMENT AGENTS OF BRITISH COLUMBIA

For Communities. For Business. For You.
www.governmentagents.gov.bc.ca

From the desk of:

- ☐ Dan Martin, Government Agent
- ☑ Rose Marie McKenzie
- ☐ Karin Nuyten

To: Rick HANSEN Foundation

Branch/ Company

Date: FEB-20/04

Fax No: ( ) 604-876-6666

 # Pages: 6 **(Incl. cover)**

Subject:

☐ **Urgent – Customer waiting**

Message:
FROM RON RiTCO

Responce Recieved Feb 20/04
Recived and Printed For Jan 5/04

Disclaimer: This facsimile is confidential. It is intended only for the use of the person to whom it is addressed. Any distribution or other use by anyone else is strictly prohibited. If you have received this facsimile in error, please telephone us immediately and destroy all attachments received with this transmission. Your co-operation is greatly appreciated.

Government Agents Office
Box 850, 7290 2 Street
Grand Forks, BC V0H 1H0
Fax: (250) 442-4317
Phone: (250) 442-4306

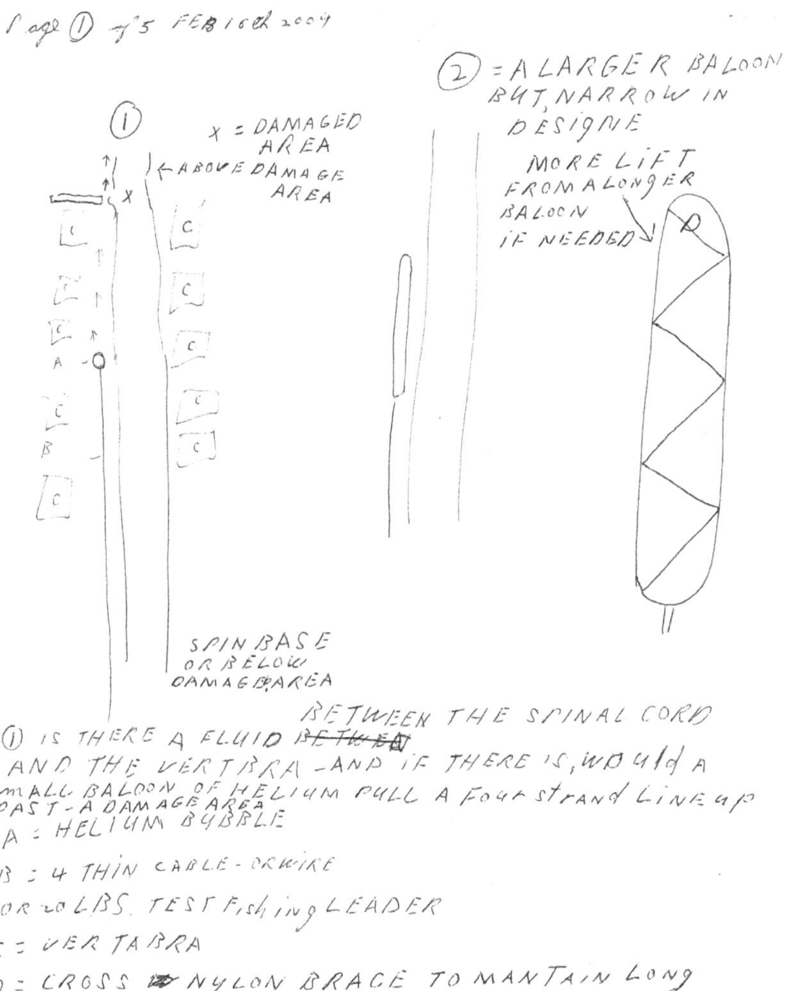

Page ① of 5 FEB 16th 2009

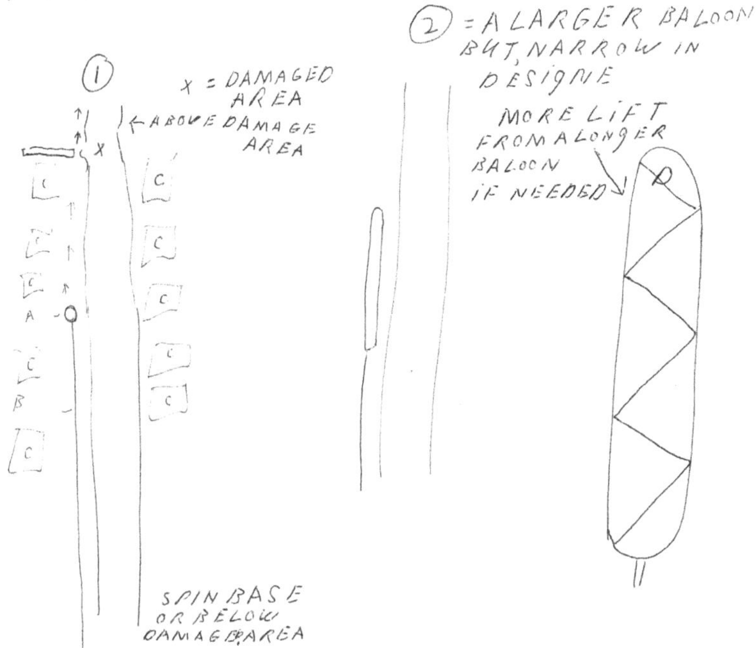
②=A LARGER BALOON
BUT, NARROW IN
DESIGNE
①
X = DAMAGED
AREA
←ABOVE DAMAGE
AREA
X
C
A
B
MORE LIFT
FROM A LONGER
BALOON
IF NEEDED
D
SPIN BASE
OR BELOW
DAMAGE AREA

① IS THERE A FLUID ~~BETWEEN~~ BETWEEN THE SPINAL CORD
AND THE VERTBRA - AND IF THERE IS, WOULD A
MALL BALOON OF HELIUM PULL A FOUR STRAND LINE UP
PAST - A DAMAGE AREA

A = HELIUM BUBBLE

B = 4 THIN CABLE - OR WIRE

OR 20 LBS. TEST FISHING LEADER

C = VERTABRA

D = CROSS NYLON BRACE TO MANTAIN LONG
NARROW SHAPE

PAGE ②
IF THE BALOON TRAVELS UPWARD WHEN
THE PERSON IS upwright
THEN WE NOW HAVE 4 LINES TO PULL
A Long-THIN JACK TO A POINT JustAbove
And just BELOW THE DAMAGED AREA

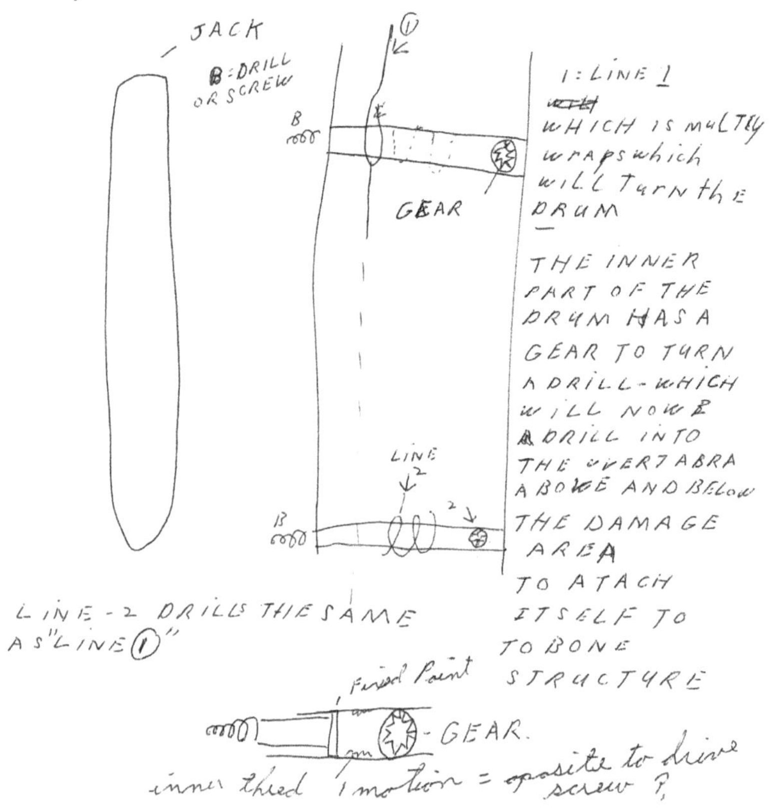

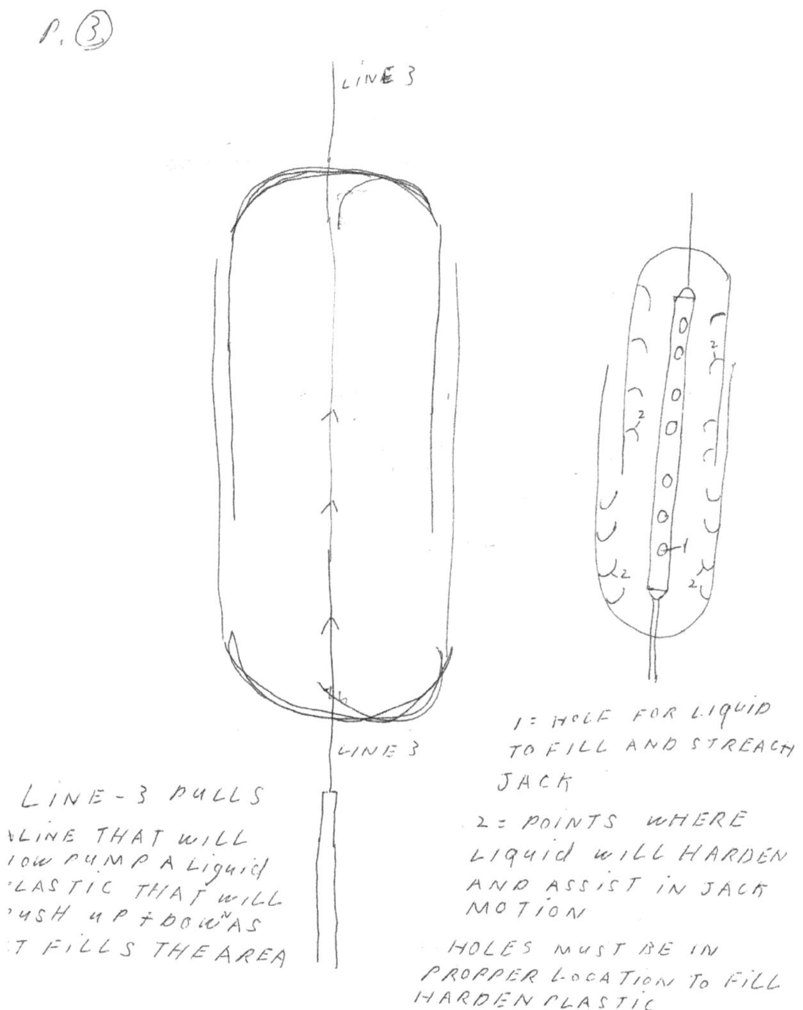
P. 3
LINE 3
LINE 3
LINE-3 PULLS
LINE THAT WILL
LOW PUMP A Liquid
LASTIC THAT WILL
USH UP + DOWN AS
T FILLS THE AREA
1 = HOLE FOR LIQUID
TO FILL AND STREACH
JACK
2 = POINTS WHERE
Liquid will HARDEN
AND ASSIST IN JACK
MOTION
HOLES MUST BE IN
PROPPER LOCATION TO FILL
HARDEN PLASTIC

P. 4 LINE (4)

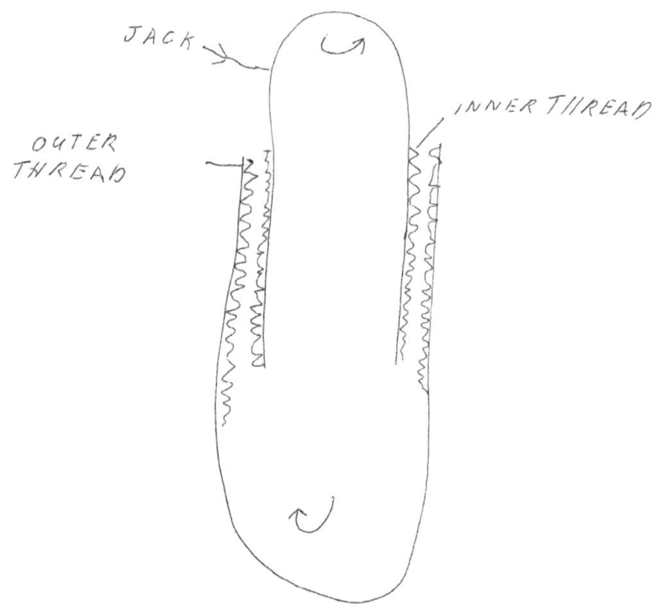

AS A FISHINGLINE COMES OUT OF A SPOOL

LINE COMES OUT

NE SPOOL ROTATES AND TURNS the THREADS
ON THE TOP AND BOTTOM OF JACK AS THE LINE IS
ULLED FROM THE TOP AND BOTTOM AT THE SAME TIME
ND LENGTHENS THE JACK.?

Page 5

IF HELIUM BALOON DOESNT work CAN THE SPACE BETWEEN THE SPINAL CORD AND THE VIRTABRA BE FILLED with A Liquid TO MAKE it work?

OR could THE BALOON "NOW BECOME" A STEEL BALL AND it would ~~pull~~ ~~AH~~ FALL DOWN WORD – MAYBEE IF THE BODY was VIBRATED it would HELP IT FALL?

Mr. Rick Hansen

Hopefully there is something in these 5 pages that will help.
Please Phone to comfirm that you have recieved this and Prior Possabilities

Ron Ritco
121 Sagamore Ave
Grand Forks B.C.
V0H-1H4
Ph. 1-250-442-0867

For Communities. For Business. For You.
www.governmentagents.gov.bc.ca

From the desk of:

- ☐ Dan Martin, Government Agent
- ☑ Rose Marie McKenzie
- ☐ Karin Nuyten

To: Rick HANSEN Foundation

Branch/ Company

Date: FEB-20/04

Fax No: ( ) 604-876-6666

 # Pages: 6 (Incl. cover)

Subject:

☐ **Urgent – Customer waiting**

Message:
FROM RON RITCO

Government Agents Office
Box 850, 7290 2 Street
Grand Forks, BC V0H 1H0
Fax: (250) 442-4317
Phone: (250) 442-4306

Disclaimer: This facsimile is confidential. It is intended only for the use of the person to whom it is addressed. Any distribution or other use by anyone else is strictly prohibited. If you have received this facsimile in error, please telephone us immediately and destroy all attachments received with this transmission. Your co-operation is greatly appreciated.

*** SUCCESSFUL TX NOTICE ***

FILE NBR : 198
SENT PAGES : 06
END TIME : FEB.20 14:00
START TIME : FEB.20 13:56

CHAPTER FORTY-SEVEN

MERRY-ANNE

God had taken my Meredith home and I was left heartbroken and alone. My brother-in-law, Mark, and his wife, Sue were staying here when they came down from Vancouver. A beautiful couple, they were building a house at Copper Ridge. Every two or three weeks they would come and work on their house with the contractors.

This one particular morning, I was on my way to town and saw a lady standing just before the bridge, hitchhiking. I stopped and she got in. She told me she was going to Whisper's for a free breakfast. I introduced myself and she told me her name was Merry-Anne. My wife had known her for many years. She was the daughter of Lee and Ken Johnson; he did stuccoing for a living and he had my brother, Ken, as his worker. Ken Johnson and my brother had stuccoed our house.

I told Merry-Anne, "If you'd like, you are welcome to come to my place and I'll make you bacon and eggs for breakfast." She laughed and said yes. I brought her home and made her breakfast, then took her home. She did part-time house cleaning for extra money, and was in need of assistance, since her rent took up most of her income.

I felt bad for her and offered her work cleaning my house. Most of my family didn't know who she was, so I would take her to family dinners now and then. There was not a lot of positive feelings for her from them, but that was okay; I felt for her, as she lived a very poor life.

As I got to know Merry-Anne, I soon found a woman with a heart beyond generous, and compassionate beyond belief. She had four cats that she loved, and the poorest people who lived in town were always welcome in her home. Some of them she hardly knew, but would tell them that they were welcome to sleep on her couch. She would also feed them and share her cigarettes. People would come and go and stay at her place for a while.

I would take her out for lunch or dinner, now and then. She would see people and ask them if they had eaten any food that day, and if they were hungry, she would share her food with them. She was always concerned about the poor, even though she herself was also poor. I would ask her if she needed anything from the store and we would go in and shop together. She had little money most of the time, and I enjoyed doing it. Merry-Anne needed cat food, cat litter and a few other things, so I would pay for it. I would also help her get her food from the food bank. I gave her a ride to the Christmas dinners that the local churches provided.

After Merry-Anne did the housekeeping at my house, I would give her some food and money to take home. I have never, in my entire life, known a lady so poor but so generous with sharing her own food and home others. There are people in this world that do not share at all, and they have so much, but Merry-Anne would share it all.

Merry-Anne has gotten very sick and may pass away. My hope is that people remember her for all of her wonderful qualities and I hope God treats her in a very special way. One of the angels on Earth!

CHAPTER FORTY-EIGHT

TRIP TO REPUBLIC WITH SETH

My grandson, Seth, and I decided to go to Republic, Washington, U.S.A. We got to the U.S. Customs office and Seth was so excited to go to to the states. I gave the border guard my passport and Seth's birth certificate along with a letter from his mom and dad giving me permission to enter the U.S.A. with my grandson.

Seth asked the border guard, "Am I in America?"

"You are now in America," the guard replied, his smile larger than life. We drove to Republic and parked across from a second-hand store. I held Seth's hand as we crossed the street, even though there was no traffic. In the middle of the street Seth said, "Grandpa, wouldn't it be something if we saw Obama?"

"Seth, that would really be something," I said as we both laughed. After the second-hand store, we went to a restaurant, as Seth needed to use the washroom. I told him that the floor of the restroom was made out of Lincoln pennies. He came out and said he has never seen a floor like that. I told him that the president on the back of all of those pennies was Abraham Lincoln, a great man who never wavered in his fight for equality.

We had a great day, and then headed back to Grand Forks. I have often wondered if I should send the story to Obama. I think he would get a good laugh as we did that day.

CHAPTER FORTY-NINE

EASTER, 2016

During Harlen and Seth's spring break from school, I asked James and Kelsey if I could take the boys for a holiday. They were happy to let me spend the time with my grandsons. We headed to Ainsworth Hot Springs and enjoyed the adventure of the hot springs and the caves. The resort treated us very well during our stay. There was a waitress with whom I traded a poem for a cup of coffee. The poem was called Princess Janette. We were having breakfast and she came over and thanked me for the poem. She had shown it to anyone who would read it, and it really made her day.

In the morning, we took the ferry and crossed the lake. We drove to Creston, where my sister Robin lives. We brought her flowers and lotto tickets. She was so excited to see the boys, and cared for them like they were her own. We truly felt at home.

From there we went to the Coeur d'alene casino and enjoyed the hot tub, the pool, and the wonderful food. The buffet was huge and all you can eat; the boys loved that. We stopped at Walmart on the way and bought Rubic's cubes, cards, soccer balls, and more, just having a great time. In the evening, the boys were in the room with the door locked and instructions not to open the door to anyone. I decided to go down to the casino to try my luck and, as usual, the casino was kind to me.

In the morning, we left. Harlen held the road map and told me which roads to turn on to take us home. He was a great navigator. We drove along and then laughed as we passed Starvation Lake and wondered if there was any fish in the lake.

The boys and I arrived at home. They had a lot of fun and so did I. Just as we entered into Canada there was a double rainbow welcoming us back home.

CHAPTER FIFTY

CURRENT

I am going to have surgery for my hip soon. I know I will be writing poems and trying to invent something new prior to my surgery. I promised myself that I would find my missing brother Clim. I've looked for answers for over twenty-five years, but that is for another book.

CHAPTER FIFTY-ONE

POEMS

The Mountie of the Day

He came and called
I will find justice
I will find your brother

He said he would search
High and low
And never quit
Even though it is cold

Year after Year
He did not quit
For he walked the path of truth

Justice was the wind
The wind in the air
He will find my brother
And bring him home

And the ones that harmed him
Will have a different home
It will be bars of steel
As price they must pay

For taking the life Of my brother Clim That day.

My Meredith

I have lived two and half lives I lived the golden dream of life I had Meredith, my wife.

I have lost my Meredith
My angel of love
I've asked God if he can please send her back to me
But that is my heart's want
And not reality
Every day I live, puts me closer to being with her again!

A Tribute to Valerie Anne

There was once a lady, her name is Valerie Anne Who gently walked upon the land.

Her smile and laughter would warm your heart
And those who knew her to feel with their hearts

A woman so poor but would share her food And give a stranger a place to sleep.

She asked many of the poor if they had eaten that day And shared her food with them that day.

I see her riding her horse And her hair blowing in the wind.

I hear the trumpets of heaven and a voice from the sky Valerie come home and to your friends now say goodbye.

And her horse now has wings and she rides into the sky And turns so gently and smiles and waves goodbye.

BUTTERFLY

November 13, 1996

Sitting under the tree
Am I five or six
Or only three
It doesn't really matter

A wild daisy in my hand
A blue sky
That covers the land
The tree at my back
Shades this moment in time

My eyes trained
On a butterfly
That is coming near
Sitting down
Trying not to move

He comes and sits
On the ground beside me
He's coming closer
Closer to the flower

But suddenly comes
And sits on my nose
I dare not move
Looking at him with
Two eyes that want to blink
And my chuckle
Heads to laughter

Away my friend the Butterfly.

The Still

November 14, 1996

On the bootlegger's trail
Upon the hill
Harry and Lindsey
Had their still

The finest copper work
Of its day
Close to a creek
Hidden away

They hauled the corn
By horse and mule
Not in the morning
But by the full moon

The fire roared
The kettle shook
The mash was ready
To be cooked

Crouched by the coil
Running through the creek
Two tin cans
Would surely meet

Drop and the shove of a cup
Let mine fill up
Only half ways
Fifty-fifty is the split of the day Laughing hard
And the crocks filling fast
Another perfect batch

On bootlegger's trail, up on the hill
It is still hidden Harry and Lindsey's still.

(These two men did in fact make moonshine in Grand Forks)

THAT WOMAN CAN DRIVE

November 14, 1996

The rifle bullets
Ripped through
What a way to make a living
Me and the old car

A hundred gallon of the finest shine
Between the doors
In this car of mine

The trunk filled with a forty-five It stopped the bullets of the F.B.I.
How was your trip down here
Quiet about the same

Siphon hoses running in every way
Hand stretched out
Waiting to be paid

The motor is running
The engine is hot
The pedal to the floor
I hear them yelling
Don't get caught

Eighty miles an hour
The border ahead
Boards and gates
Flying overhead

Over the bridge
Onto Carson Road again
No lights on
The moon over head

Did you girls have a good card game
Yes, dear, but tomorrow night
We'll be playing again

(Mrs. Pennoyer running Moonshine across the border to Capone)

BUS DRIVER

November 15, 1996

Running for the bus
Like a leopard
After its prey

Nothing is more important
At this moment
I hear the air brakes
I've been saved

Like an eagle
Soaring through the sky
Always watching the nest
With one eye

He knows them one
He knows them all
He shifts a gear
And carrys on

Good morning Mr. Carter
Good morning, Jess
Good morning Mr. Carter
Good morning, James

The bus is filled
On its usual route
And all are delivered
Without a thought

He rules the bus
With respect and ease All the parents
Their minds are at ease.
(Terrie Carter, the kid's school bus driver)

THE THREE OF THEM

November 15, 1996

As they stretched out, down the road
Where in life will they go

Rick is in charge and always ahead
Ron in the middle and growing taller again

Terri is last of course, she always is
Watching the trees, the birds and things

Ron stops for a moment
To pick up a dime
Rick is ahead of me
And doing just fine

They stretched out, down the road
From spring, to fall and through the snow
Where in life will they go

The day came when it ended
And the line was gone
In their lives they carry on

Who is first, second or third
Is immaterial now
But all three of them
Walk so proud

Where in life will they go Only the three of them Only know.

(Rick, Ron and Terri going to school)

STAR

November 15, 1996

In the sky, the stars above
Is there a star, a star of love

Does it shine forever in time
Or in my eyes, when I'm in love

Does it shine, from my eyes
To yours

Does it shine to remind, my mind
That I am only yours

Does it shine for this soul in time
To find a love, a love of mine

Does it shine for the universe to see
That my love is only for thee

Does this star, so far above
Tell the worlds, we're in love

Does this star so far above
Does this star, the star of love
Does this star
Forever shine our love
(A poem about Meredith and I)

FARMER

November 15, 1996

In his arms, stacked high
Like firewood in size
He grew potatoes
With all his pride

October's wind
It covered us all
It was harvest time
In the fall

The tractor strained
The crop was good Load after load
He hauled in wood

When all was done
And stored in time
We hurried to fields
One more time

Planting rye
For a cover crop
He worked through night
He didn't stop
The final frost
Was here to stay
On to the packing house
The very next day

Thousands of tons
Before his eyes
He said, that'll feed the people
He smiled with
All his pride
(I worked for John Ogloff, he was the best farmer in Grand Forks)

MEREDITH

November 15, 1996

She danced on the wind
Of the evening sun
She was a gift
A gift of love

Heaven's trumpets
Cried out with pain
And on earth
Meredith was her name

With god as her weapon
And her heart had no lies
There was nothing
She could not in time conquer

Heartache was swift
To strike the first blow
But in the end, she found me
That is all she had to know

Heaven's trumpets
Cried out in pain
And on earth
Meredith was her name

I've learned through time
That she is so fine
Meredith is her name

Heaven blow your trumpets
But leave her here with me
One day you
Might blow your trumpets for me

MOM

November 16, 1996

(For my mother-in-law Jean Dow)

Opening the back door
A broom whistled
Over my head

With lightning speed
The swat of a broom
She had them cornered
In the corner of the room

They wouldn't fight each other
They would be lucky to escape
Broom flashing with accuracy
And speed

She thrashed those boys
Down to their knees
Out, out of my kitchen

With ouches and ouches
They headed for the door
Arms and legs everywhere
The speed of the broom whirled in the air

Rolling and struggling
And trying to stand
She had the broom
And she was in command

Out of my kitchen
No fighting allowed
Then both passed me
At the speed of sound

She looked at me and smiled
Oh, hi Ron
Mom is it safe to come in
(beating the boys)

DINNER

November 16, 1996

(Dad and I working at Focure Needles Ferry-I'm 16 years old)

The oven door was open
Invited for dinner
Be at the house at three
Our Volkswagen van
Had no heater or fan

We stood at the door
In two feet of snow
And thanked god
For all the warm clothes

We walked into their humble home
Walls of rock and floor of stone
Not undressing
Of assorted kinds
She added sugar
And raisins so fine
The oven door was open
And there sat the cat
She moved him out
And put the muffins in

The muffins were ready
Time to take them out
They were hot and good
But awkward to eat
Wearing mitts

The oven quickly cooled
And the cat
Jumped back into the oven
For they were dressed the same

The cook stove roared
But almost in vain
We ate bear and goat
In a delicious way

She ground the grain
The only warm spot
In the entire room

Your invited for dinner
Be at the house at three
I will always remember
That cat in the oven
Happy as can be!

ROSE
November 17, 1996
(Meredith)

A woman is a rose
That a man's heart
Can only hold

The pedals unveil
In perfect form
She is love
And warmth

She is strong and gentle
Both at the same time
She is love
She is mine

She is a fragrance
Pure and strong
She is my love
And can do no wrong

She slowly opens
In the heart of mine
Time and days
Keep going by

She is a rose
Of a special kind
In my heart
She's always alive

Time comes
Time goes
A woman is a rose
That my heart
Can only hold.

LITTLE MAN

November 17, 1996

(See Leprechaun in the Book-Sandy's Art)

Standing on the lawn
Three, four inches tall
His hat was brimmed
With a buckle of brass

The same at his waist
And his shoe buckles shone
As he walked across the lawn

He saw me watching him
He froze in his tracks
Our eyes met
How long would it last

His suit was pressed
In perfect form
But I remember the story
Of folklore

Keeping my eyes open
He started to walk
Your trying to trick me
Aint you my little friend

My eyes are strained
As he walked along
I blinked my eyes
And he was gone

I ran to the lawn
And looked behind the tree
Did I see
What I thought I had seen

GIFT

November 17, 1996

A child is a gift
A gift to the world
A gift to an endless maze
I hope the gift
The gift is strong
The gift is good
And carries on
The gift is a girl
The girl gives a gift
A gift to carry on
The gift is held
In precious arms
The gift will carry on
The gift is given
The gift is a boy
The gift is strong
To carry on
The gift is given
Always to give away
To build the world
In a better way
(A child, is a gift to the world)

POET

November 18, 1996

I am a poet
In this day and time
In the walls of this book
I hope you will find

Something humorous
Hopefully nothing sad
Something to make you see
The true world at hand

I am not here to judge you all
I am not here to condemn at all
I hope you see
What is really there to see

I sit in the barn
With wood stove to my left
I'm armed with a pen
And my dog is red
He sits on a blanket
And rests his head
Not caring what his master
Is doing with a pen
My book is on a table
My coffee cup is near
My fiery love
My gorgeous wife
Is very near

I am a poet
In this day and time I hope you read
This book of mine.
$17.95
November 19, 1996
(Guaranteed a Place in Heaven)

Send- $17.95
I guarantee you a seat in heaven
Forever, for all time
If you want your own mansion
It'll cost you only
Another twenty-five
Not a problem
I'll make the walls of gold
Ceiling of sapphires
And yes of course
You'll never get old
Nothing wrong with young women
Running up and down the hall
Only twenty dollars a head, that's all
Yes, man, it's true, it's true
Muscle builder
Lots of young men for you
The more you buy
The better deal you will get
Folks, Folks
Everybody get back in line
It's only $17.95

KISS

November 19, 1996

(Meredith and Ron)

I kissed her lips
And she kissed mine
The seed of love
Was planted in our lives

Our eyes looked
Into each other's eyes
As we looked
Beyond our lives

It was that kiss
It was the best
And love
Would do the rest

It took control
Of our hearts and our souls
And always together
In our life we go

Years and time
Keep rolling by
We're still together
Doing just fine

All around us
They've come and gone
We live in our own world
And we carry on

TEENAGE DAUGHTER

January 3, 1997

Oh God, please give me
A cup of coffee, a cigarette
And five minutes alone
Then I will face her
Fearless and alone
My daughter is Fifteen
And armed with words
At the farthest end of the table
I dare to sit
I look out the window
And enjoy these last few seconds of peace
There is no need
To drop a match
In a barrel of gunpowder
The fuse is already lit
Oh god, please give me
A cup of coffee, a cigarette
And five minutes alone
She slowly turns
And looks at me
And says in her usual way What the hell is the matter With you today!

The River of Life

January 5, 1997

Her life flows
In the river of life
She is sometimes wrong
But more often right
She has a soft
And gentle smile
She is calm
She is still
There are places
Where you cannot cross
In the rapids
You will be lost
You cannot change her
She is right
She has planted
Five seeds to grow
On the journey home
When the seeds
Are caught on the shore She returns them
To the river of life.

Faller

January 3, 1997

Beaten all to hell
Crawling from under the tree
Hit with chunks of ice
And parts and pieces of trees
Still alive,
And crawling through the snow
Off to another tree he goes
Hands frozen
From the snow
From tree to tree
He carrys on
Sandwiches frozen
Like rock hard pucks
Good luck eating lunch
Quitting time comes
Time to go
Home is the place
To rest and thaw
Morning light breaks
Your ready again
Back in the bush

The bush again.

LOVE

January 6, 1997

She touched my hand
My heart quivered
With shyness
She looked at me
With her eyes
And had control of me
But when she smiled
She knew all the while
I had no control
Over me
Her lips quivered
As her words
Hypnotized me
No strength to run
No power to move
Her love overpowered My every move.

SEPTEMBER 11TH

January 12, 2001

Two planes in the sky
Have judged
Who will live
And who will die
Two mighty towers
Fell to dust
Thousands of people
Gave out a cry Why me?
Is it time to die
But above the dust
And rubble below
There souls come together
And see there bodys below
There souls unite
In a mighty strength
They are peacefully calm
A call from heaven
Gives them a direction to go
The old and young
Are helped along
To heaven's home
The gates of heaven
Open wide
They are all called in
Before the doors are slammed
And nineteen souls Are told to leave For this is not your home.

SISTERS

FEBRUARY 23, 2002

Four of the most beautiful sisters
That the world has ever known
One with a diamond ring
I have had the pleasure
For one to hold
And the four sisters greet the rising sun
As it warms the earth
They are alike as one
Life tries to separate them
But always loses

To the strength they hold
As they are four in one
And one in four
Their voices and ways
Are like the sun shining
Everyday
Morning light
Stars at night
The sisters
Stand together
Throughout life And if one should slip and fall The others will stand tall.

TODAY

February 24, 2002

She reached out
And our hands met
The touch of our hands
Was a special event
The milky way
And the dancing northern lights
The moon shone bright
As to say
Everything is right
The moment the touch
Was a surge of love
Feelings dancing in our hearts
Trembling breathing
And shyness in our words
As we both said
I like you a lot
These feelings have no control
As our lips touched
We were out of control
Oh love has taken us away In a world of own Today.

GOLD

February 25, 2002

Gretsky chose the men
To play the Olympic games
Every player upon the team
Had the want of the Olympic dream
The games were battles
Fought inside each player
Saying to themselves
I know we can win
Game after game
The battle raged
Goal after goal
Black bullets tore through the net
The will of the best
Are here to win
Gretsky stood and spoke
We will stand tall
Mario Lemeux and Bullet Joe
And all the great players
That we know
Came together for us all
Gold is what echoed
In their minds
Gold gave their beaten bodies
More strength in inside
It is the team of teams
The coach aims
He fires
A wall of hockey strikes
Armed by the best
Skate across the ice
They shoot they score
For all of Canada
They hold the stick tight

We cheer them on
As we have never
Cheered before
Gold for the Canadian Warriors Was always
In their hands!

THE WAY HOME

March 3, 2002

Man is the only one
Who ask the question
That can't be answered

The one who wants to know
But doesn't have enough time to learn everything
The one wants to conquer the world
The one that wants to save the world

And now he looks in awe
And knows he never should have
Ever done anything at all

Create the situation
That you can only save
Did the Roman Empire ever leave
Or in a future date
It now still remains

What is right, what is wrong
Are only memories
For an unsung song

I can go back to the future
Tomorrow with ease
And change it meticulously
To a perfect way

But like my brother said
The journey home is a long one

You should dance to the music
And beat your dream
So said the chief
Relax a little
Your future
Has just begun

CONCLUSION

As I stated at the beginning of this book, I have had some of the most unexplainable and unbelievable events happen in my life, and Meredith shared them with me, we were one! One love, forever, in life and in death!

Thank God and thank you to my daughter-in-law, Kelsey, who can read my horrible writing and making this book a reality and a possibility.

A huge thank you to Mike for his tireless editing and organizing and time he spent to make this book happen.

Thank you to my sister-in-law Sandy for creating the art for this book. I know she has put her heart and soul into her paintings.

I am hoping my inventions have done the world some good. I hope my book of poems is enjoyable, and I hope my hundreds of lyrics become songs one day.

I hope for love and laughter for all of my family, one and all!

Ronnie Ritco

CPSIA information can be obtained
at www.ICGtesting.com
Printed in the USA
LVHW070318010619
619805LV00001B/1/P